MAX V. MATHEWS
with the
collaboration
of
Joan E. Miller
F. R. Moore
J. R. Pierce
and J. C. Risset

The
Technology
of
Computer
Music

The
Technology
of
Computer
Music

THE M.I.T. PRESS
Massachusetts Institute of Technology
Cambridge, Massachusetts, and London, England

Second printing, January 1974

ISBN 0 262 13050 5
Library of Congress catalog card number: 69–12754

Printed and bound in the United States of America

Contents

3. Music V Manual

1 Fundamentals

Introduction

This book is intended for people who plan to use computers for sound processing. Present users range from engineers and physicists concerned with speech and acoustics to musicians and phoneticians concerned with sound synthesis and speech production and perception. The widely varied technical and mathematical background of this audience makes it hard to select a technical level for this presentation. Some experience with a computer language such as FØRTRAN will be assumed, though it could be obtained at the time this material is studied.

Occasionally a satisfactory explanation of some point requires mathematics at the level of a graduate curriculum in electrical engineering. These mathematical sections have been quarantined and marked with an asterisk. Although the mathematical material adds essential understanding of sound processing, the rest of the book is intended to be comprehensible without it. The implications of the mathematics are usually given in elementary terms in other sections. Also, Appendix B lists the main relationships required for mathematical background.

Chapter 1 covers some fundamentals that are basic to all computer sound processing—the representation of sounds as numbers, the underlying processes of sampling and quantizing a sound wave, the approximations and errors that are inherent in sampling and quantizing, the operation of digital-to-analog and analog-to-digital converters, the construction of smoothing filters, the storage and manipulation of sound waves in numerical form, and, last, an introductory look at the computer programming for sound processing which is the central subject of the rest of the book.

Numerical Representation of Functions of Time

Sound can be considered as a changing or time-varying pressure in the air. Its subjective characteristics, how it "sounds," depend on the specific way the pressure varies. For example, a tone with a definite pitch A above middle C has a periodic pressure variation that repeats itself 440 times each second. A constant pressure is heard as silence.

Since the essence of the sound depends on the nature of the variations in pressure, we will describe a sound wave by a pressure function p(t). The p stands for pressure, the t for time, and the parentheses indicate that pressure is a function of time; in other words, pressure changes as time goes on. The term p(t) will represent the pressure function of time or, more briefly, the pressure function.

One way to describe pressure functions is to draw a picture or graph showing how they vary with time. Two simple examples are shown in Fig. 1. Figure 1a shows a constant pressure heard as silence. Figure 1b shows a sinusoidal variation that repeats itself each 1/500 second. Thus the pitch will be slightly below C (524 Hz). The time scale is labeled in thousandths of a second. The variations are very rapid compared with the times in which we schedule our lives. The pressure wave cannot be described as a single quantity or number. Its whole history must be drawn, and there is an infinite variety of ways in which it can change from millisecond to millisecond.

The pressure is shown increasing or decreasing around zero pressure. Actually the variations are around the pressure of the atmosphere, about 15 pounds per square inch. However, atmospheric pressure is essentially constant and produces no sound. The variations are small compared to the atmospheric pressure: A very loud sound would change from 15 to 15.001 pounds per square inch. The minuteness of this variation indicates the great sensitivity of our ears.

All sounds have a *pressure function* and any sound can be produced by generating its pressure function. Thus if we can develop a pressure source capable of producing any pressure function, it will be capable of producing any sound, including speech, music, and noise. A digital computer, plus a program, plus a digital-to-analog converter, plus a loudspeaker come close to meeting this capability.

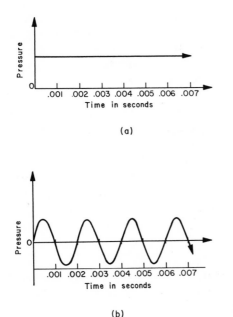

(a)

Fig. 1. Simple pressure functions: (a) silence; (b) 500-Hz sinusoid.

(b)

In the past most sounds have originated from the vibrations and movements of natural objects—human vocal cords, violin strings, colliding automobiles. The nature of these sounds is determined by and limited by the particular objects. However, in the last 50 years the loudspeaker has been developed as a general sound source. It produces a pressure function by means of the vibrations of a paper cone actuated by a coil of wire in a magnetic field. The movement of the cone as a function of time, and hence the resulting pressure function, are determined by the electric voltage (as a function of time) applied to the coil.

Loudspeakers are not perfect: they distort all sounds slightly, and some sounds are hard to produce. However, the almost universal range of sounds they generate in a satisfactory way is demonstrated by the range of sounds that can be played on phonograph records and on radios. Loudspeakers are sound sources of almost unlimited richness and potential.

To drive a loudspeaker and produce a desired pressure function, an electric voltage function of time must be applied to its coil. Exchanging the problem of generating a pressure function for generating a voltage function might seem to offer little gain. However, very versatile methods exist for producing electric functions.

One popular method of generating a great variety of voltage functions is the phonograph record. The minute wiggles in the grooves on the record are converted into a motion function of the needle on the pickup. The wiggles are a space function, but this space function is converted to a time function by the turntable, which moves the groove past the needle at a particular speed. The motion function of the needle is converted to a voltage function in one of a number of well-known ways. The voltage, after amplification, is applied to the loudspeaker.

The value of the phonograph as a source of voltage functions is that a wiggle of almost any shape can be cut in the groove. If one had a minute chisel, grooves for new sounds could be cut by hand. However, the computer can accomplish an equivalent result by a much easier process.

Sampling and Quantizing

The pressure functions that we hear as sound are generated by applying the corresponding voltage functions to a loudspeaker. How can voltage functions be produced from the numbers in a computer? The process is shown in Fig. 2. Numbers stored in the computer memory are successively transferred to a digital-to-analog converter.

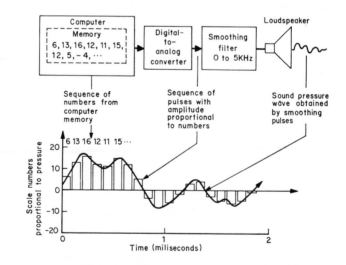

Fig. 2. Computer-to-pressure conversion.

For each number the converter generates a pulse of voltage whose amplitude equals the number. These pulses are shown on the graph in the lower part of Fig. 2. The square corners of the pulses are smoothed with a filter (low-pass filter) to produce the smooth voltage function drawn through the pulses in Fig. 2. This voltage, supplied to the loudspeaker, produces the desired pressure wave.

We will discuss later the electrical details of the digital-to-analog converter and the smoothing filter, and analyze the errors quantitatively. Here we would like to give some physical intuition about the process. From inspection of Fig. 2, it seems evident that a great variety of time functions can be generated from the right numbers. Each number simply gives the value of the function at one instant in time. Practically, the computer can produce any set of numbers and hence any time function. However, some functions are more difficult to produce than others, and certain approximations are involved in producing any function. It is important to understand the nature of these approximations in order to use the computer as an effective sound source. *Sampling* and *quantizing* are the two approximations involved in representing a continuous function by a set of numbers.

A continuous function of time can change at every instant in time. The numbers, by contrast, are converted to pulses which are constant for a given duration, called the pulse width or sampling time. In Fig. 2, there are 10 pulses each millisecond, so the sampling time is 1/10,000 sec. It is often convenient to talk about the sampling rate that is 1/(sampling time). Thus a sampling time of 1/10,000 sec corresponds to a rate of 10,000 samples per second.

Intuitively it seems that, if we make the sampling time very small, the pulses will be a good approximation to the continuous function as illustrated in Fig. 3a, and if we make the sampling time large, as in Fig. 3b, we will get a poor approximation. Of course, the approximation depends on the function too. More pulses are needed to approximate a rapidly changing function than a slowly changing one. The rapidly changing function is best thought of as having higher frequencies than the slowly changing function. Thus a higher sampling rate, and hence more pulses, and hence more numbers, will be required to approximate high-bandwidth (hi fi) sound than low-fidelity sound.

Mathematically it has been shown that R pulses per second are needed to approximate perfectly a function with a bandwidth $R/2$ cycles per second. Thus, to approximate a high-fidelity sound with a bandwidth of 15,000 Hz, we require 30,000 samples per second, or a sampling time of 1/30,000 sec.

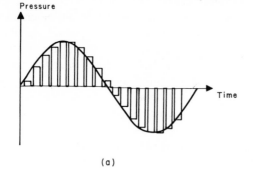

(a)

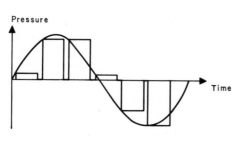

(b)

Fig. 3. Example of various sampling rates: (a) high sampling rate; (b) low sampling rate.

We can now begin to appreciate the huge task facing the computer. For each second of high-fidelity sound, it must supply 30,000 numbers to the digital-to-analog converter. Indeed, it must put out numbers steadily at a rate of 30,000 per second. Modern computers are capable of this performance, but only if they are expertly used. We can also begin to appreciate the inherent complexity of pressure functions producing sound. We said such a pressure could not be described by one number; now it is clear that a few minutes of sound require millions of numbers.

The second approximation is called quantizing. The numbers in computers contain only a certain number of digits. The numbers in the Fig. 2 computer have only two digits. Thus, for example, all the pulse amplitudes between 12.5 and 13.5 must be represented by the number 13. Of course we could build a larger computer that could handle three-digit numbers. This machine could represent 12.5 exactly. However, it would have to approximate all the amplitudes between 12.45 and 12.55 by 12.5. Furthermore, the more digits, the more expensive will be the computer.

The quantizing errors are closely equivalent to the noise and distortion that are produced by phonographs, tape recorders, amplifiers, and indeed all sound-generating equipment. Their magnitude can be estimated in terms of signal-to-noise ratios or percentage distortions. The approximate signal-to-noise ratio inherent in a given number of digits equals

$$\frac{\text{Maximum number expressible with the digits}}{\text{Maximum error in representing any number}}$$

For example, with two-decimal digits, the maximum number is 99 and the maximum error is .5. The signal-to-noise ratio is

$$\frac{99}{.5} \simeq 200 \quad \text{or} \quad 46\,\text{dB}$$

Three-decimal digits would correspond to a signal-to-noise ratio of 999/.5, or 66 dB. This ratio is as good as very high-quality audio equipment. Three-decimal digits would be a very small number of digits for most computers; hence quantizing errors are not critical. Sampling rate, by contrast, is often critical.

Most computers use binary rather than decimal numbers. The same method can be used to estimate quantizing errors. For example, 10-digit binary numbers can express the decimal integers from 0 to 1023. Hence the equivalent signal-to-noise ratio is 1023/.5, or about 66 dB. Typically, 10- to 12-binary-digit numbers are used for sound generation.

The limit to the quantizing errors is usually the digital-to-analog converter rather than the computer. Computers with an accuracy of 12 to 36 digits or more are standard. Converters with accuracy beyond 12 digits are difficult to make. Twelve digits would correspond to a signal-to-noise ratio of 78 dB. Although this ratio may seem more than sufficient, its quantizing noise is occasionally objectionable when very soft sounds are generated, or when a peculiar interaction arises between sounds and noise. Thus it seems prudent to use at least 12 digits.

Foldover Errors

The generation of voltage functions from quantized samples is a practical, powerful, and useful method when coupled to modern computers. Most of this book is concerned with applications of this method. In order to use the method, its errors and limitations must be understood and avoided. A mathematical analysis of the errors is given later in this chapter. Since the quantizing noise is similar to noise in other apparatus, it usually causes no unexpected trouble. However, sampling produces a frequency distortion called *foldover*, which can generate surprising and unwanted frequencies. Because of foldover's insidious nature, we will present an intuitive discussion here, in addition to an analysis later.

The limitations of sampling in reproducing waveforms that contain very high frequencies can be illustrated graphically. Figure 4a shows the sampling of a periodic sequence of short pulses. We see that only one out of the four pulses shown overlaps a sampling time, and hence in the figure all samples but one are zero in amplitude. The sampling of the regular sequence of pulses produces samples spaced much farther apart in time than the pulses are.

Figure 4b is another illustration of the defects of sampling. Here sampling of a square wave produces pairs of positive samples separated by single negative samples.

Thus sampling a waveform can produce samples that represent the

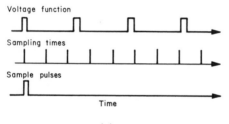

(a)

Fig. 4. (a) Sampling a function that has narrow pulses; (b) sampling a square-wave function.

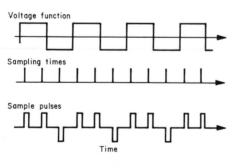

(b)

waveform poorly. This happens when the voltage function has frequencies higher than R/2 Hz, where R is the sampling rate. This is the case for the voltage functions and sampling rates shown in Fig. 4.

When the voltage function contains frequencies higher than R/2 Hz, these higher frequencies are reduced, and the resulting sound is heard somewhere in the range 0 to R/2 Hz. For example, if the sampling rate is 30,000 Hz and we generate samples of a sine wave at a frequency of 25,000 Hz

$$\sin (2\pi \cdot 25,000 \cdot t)$$

the resulting voltage function out of the low-pass filter (smoothing filter, Fig. 2) will be a sine wave at 5000 Hz

$$\sin (2\pi \cdot 5000 \cdot t)$$

More generally, if we generate samples of a sine wave at F Hz, where F is greater than R/2, the resulting frequency will be

$$F_{fold} = R - F$$

The frequency F is reflected or folded by the sampling frequency; hence the term foldover.

Why does foldover occur? Some physical feeling is suggested by Fig. 5. Here we have diagrammed the example discussed above, of a 25,000-Hz sine wave sampled at 30,000 Hz. The samples of the 25,000-Hz wave are shown as points, and the actual numbers are

$$1, .5, -.5, -1, -.5, .5, 1, .5, \ldots$$

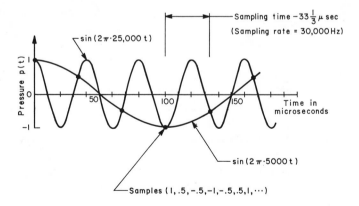

Fig. 5. Example of high-frequency (25,000 Hz) and foldover frequency (5000 Hz) resulting from low sampling rate (30,000 Hz).

A 5000-Hz sine wave is also shown, and it also passes through the same sample points. In other words, the 5000-Hz wave will have the identical samples and therefore the identical numbers as the 25,000-Hz wave. When the pulses produced by these numbers are put into the low-pass filter, a 5000-Hz wave will come out, because the low-pass filter passes low frequencies and attenuates high frequencies.

The essential point in the example is the identity of the samples of the 25,000-Hz and 5000-Hz waves. Hence from the samples there is no way to distinguish between these frequencies. No computer program or electric filter or other device can separate identical objects. For practical purposes, the digital-to-analog converter and smoothing filter will always be designed to interpret the samples as a 5000-Hz wave, that is, a wave between 0 and R/2 Hz. Thus one must be willing to accept this frequency in the sound, or one must avoid generating samples of a 25,000-Hz wave (in general, a wave with frequencies greater than R/2 Hz).

The example chosen was simple in order that the graph could be easily seen and the numbers easily computed. But the relation $F_{fold} = R - F$ holds for sine waves generally. More complex periodic waves can be decomposed into individual harmonics and the foldover frequency calculated separately for each harmonic.

Foldover also occurs from multiples of the sampling rate. Components of $\pm R \pm F$, $\pm 2R \pm F$, $\pm 3R \pm F$, etc., are produced by the digital-to-analog converter. However, in most cases only $R - F$ is troublesome.

We will next illustrate the sound of foldover with two examples. Suppose a sine wave with continuously increasing frequency (glissando) is sampled. What will be heard? As the frequency increases from 0 to 15,000 Hz, an increasing frequency going from 0 to 15,000 Hz will be heard. But as the frequency increases from 15,000 to 30,000 Hz, a *decreasing* frequency (30,000 − F) will be heard, going from 15,000 to 0 Hz. This is usually a shock! If we persist in raising the frequency and proceed from 30,000 to 45,000 Hz, the resulting sound will go upward from 0 to 15,000 Hz (−30,000 + F).

If we generate a complex tone with a high pitch and many harmonics, the higher harmonics will fold over and appear at unwanted frequencies. For example, the fifth harmonic of a 3000-Hz tone will occur at 15,000 Hz. That is the highest frequency that is not folded at a 30,000-Hz sampling rate. The sixth harmonic (18,000 Hz) will be generated at 12,000 Hz and thus add to the fourth harmonic. The ninth harmonic (27,000 Hz) will appear at the fundamental frequency, 3000 Hz.

In this example the fundamental frequency is a divisor of the sampling rate. In this case the folded higher harmonics fall at exactly the frequencies of the lower-frequency harmonics, thus producing a slight distortion of the spectrum shape. Such distortion is seldom objectionable. However, the sampling rate is not usually an exact multiple of the fundamental frequency, and the folded harmonics will not fall on lower harmonics. For a tone whose fundamental is 3100 Hz, the sixth harmonic (18,600 Hz) will fall at 11,400 Hz between the third harmonic (9300 Hz) and the fourth harmonic (12,400 Hz). At the least, the tone quality will be much changed. At the worst, dissonance that resembles intermodulation distortion will be generated.

The practical conclusion from this discussion of foldover is: avoid generating samples of waveforms whose frequencies are higher than half the sampling rate.

*Mathematical Analysis of Sampling

We will present a version of the sampling theorem in this section to show that frequency-limited functions can be represented by a sequence of numbers, and to show what errors are made by sampling functions that are not strictly frequency limited. The main result is: functions containing frequencies between 0 and $R/2$ can be exactly represented by R samples per second. The sampling of functions that are not frequency limited produces foldover errors whose magnitude can be calculated. Also errors introduced by the smoothing filter can be calculated. Quantizing errors will not be considered: each sample will be assumed to be exactly represented by a number with infinite decimal places.

Figure 6 presents a block diagram of a sampling and desampling process which we will use to analyze sampling. A time function

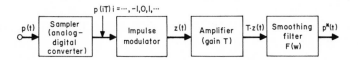

Fig. 6. Conceptual block diagram of sampling-desampling process.

$p(t)$, $-\infty < t < \infty$, is sampled. The analog-to-digital converter produces a sequence of numbers $p(iT)$, $i = \ldots, -1, 0, 1, 2, \ldots$, equal to $p(t)$ at the sampling times iT. The sampling interval is T, and the sampling rate $R = 1/T$.

The desampling process consists of an "impulse" modulator, an amplifier, and a smoothing filter. The output of the modulator is a sequence of impulses z(t) whose areas are respectively proportional to p(iT). Thus

$$z(t) = \sum_{i=-\infty}^{+\infty} \delta(t - iT)p(iT) \tag{1}$$

where $\delta(t)$ is a unit impulse at time $t = 0$. In actual practice, the impulse modulator is well approximated by a pulse modulator producing pulses of finite width. The impulses are smoothed by an ideal low-pass filter, having unity gain from 0 to R/2 Hz and zero gain above R/2 Hz. Such a filter is unrealizable but can be well approximated by filters that can be constructed.

The output of the smoothing filter $p^*(t)$ should equal or closely approximate $p(t)$. The essential result is simply that, for any frequency-limited $p(t)$, $p(t) = p^*(t)$. This result not only establishes that any frequency-limited function can be generated from *samples* but also gives a recipe for sampling any *frequency-limited* function. Thus a basis is built for both sampling and desampling. Although one frequently works with only sampling (for sound analysis) or only desampling (for sound synthesis), the complete sampling-desampling process is conceptually necessary to establish the validity and accuracy of either process.

In addition to being frequency limited, $p(t)$ must satisfy certain additional requirements of a more subtle mathematical nature. In general we will ignore these qualifications here, with apologies to the mathematicians. Functions obtained from sound waves satisfy these qualifications.

The function $p(t)$ can be expressed as the inverse Fourier transform

$$p(t) = \frac{1}{2\pi} \int_{-\infty}^{+\infty} P(\omega)e^{j\omega t} \, d\omega \tag{2}$$

where the spectrum of $p(t)$ is $P(\omega)$. If $p(t)$ is frequency limited to half the sampling rate R, then $P(\omega) = 0$ for $|\omega| \geq \frac{1}{2}\omega_0$ where $\omega_0 = 2\pi R$. A

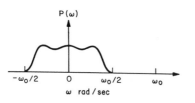

Fig. 7. Typical frequency-limited spectrum.

sketch of such a P(ω) is shown in Fig. 7. The output of the impulse modulator may be written as the product

$$z(t) = m(t) \cdot p(t)$$

where m(t) is a sequence of unit impulses at the sampling rate

$$m(t) = \sum_{j=-\infty}^{+\infty} \delta(t - iT)$$

as shown in Fig. 8. The spectrum M(ω) of m(t) can be formally

m(t)

$-2T$ $-T$ 0 T $2T$ $3T$
t sec

Fig. 8. Sampling impulses.

represented[1] as a sequence of impulses in the frequency domain

$$M(\omega) = \frac{2\pi}{T} \sum_{n=-\infty}^{+\infty} \delta(\omega - n\omega_0) \qquad (3)$$

as shown in Fig. 9.

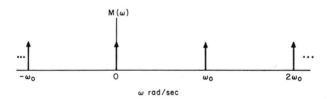

M(ω)

$-\omega_0$ 0 ω_0 $2\omega_0$
ω rad/sec

Fig. 9. Spectrum of sampling impulses.

[1] This spectrum may be formally derived from the Fourier series analysis of m(t), which yields

$$m(t) = \frac{1}{T} + \frac{2}{T} \sum_{n=1}^{\infty} \cos n\omega_0 t$$

The spectrum of $\cos n\omega_0 t$ is

$$\pi[\delta(\omega - n\omega_0) + \delta(\omega + n\omega_0)]$$

Hence the spectrum of m(t) may be computed as the sum of spectrums of $\cos n\omega_0 t$ terms

$$M(\omega) = \frac{2\pi}{T} \sum_{n=-\infty}^{+\infty} \delta(\omega - n\omega_0)$$

Using the convolution theorem, the spectrum $Z(\omega)$ of $z(t)$ may be written in terms of $M(\omega)$ and $P(\omega)$ as the integral

$$Z(\omega) = \frac{1}{2\pi} \int_{-\infty}^{+\infty} M(\alpha)P(\omega - \alpha)\,d\alpha \qquad (4)$$

Substituting the series for $M(\omega)$

$$Z(\omega) = \frac{1}{T} \sum_{n=-\infty}^{+\infty} \int_{-\infty}^{+\infty} \delta(\alpha - n\omega_0)P(\omega - \alpha)\,d\alpha$$

which, because of the nature of the impulse function, simplifies to

$$Z(\omega) = \frac{1}{T} \sum_{n=-\infty}^{+\infty} P(\omega - n\omega_0) \qquad (5)$$

The spectrum $P^*(\omega)$ of the output $p^*(t)$ is $Z(\omega)$ times the product of the amplification T and the transfer function $F(\omega)$ of the smoothing filter

$$P^*(\omega) = F(\omega) \sum_{n=-\infty}^{+\infty} P(\omega - n\omega_0) \qquad (6)$$

Equation 6 is the basic result and holds for both frequency-limited and frequency-nonlimited $P(\omega)$'s. It says that $P^*(\omega)$ contains the sum of $P(\omega)$ spectra which have been shifted by $n\omega_0$. Let us examine $P^*(\omega)$ for the frequency-limited case.

Figure 10 shows a sketch of $T \cdot Z(\omega)$ for the $P(\omega)$ shown in Fig. 7. Since $P(\omega) = 0$ for $|\omega| \geq \omega_0/2$, the sum of shifted $P(\omega)$ spectra gives

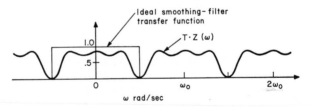

Fig. 10. Spectrum of $T \cdot Z(\omega)$ and smoothing-filter transfer function with frequency-limited function.

copies of the $P(\omega)$ spectra centered at $\ldots, -\omega_0, 0, \omega_0, 2\omega_0, \ldots$ rad/sec. If the smoothing transfer function $F(\omega)$ is such that $F(\omega) = 1$ for $|\omega| < \omega_0/2$, and $F(\omega) = 0$ for $|\omega| \geq \omega_0/2$ as shown in Fig. 10, then $P^*(\omega)$ is simply the center hump of $T \cdot Z(\omega)$. Geometrically it is easy to see that $P^*(\omega) = P(\omega)$ and therefore that $p(t) = p^*(t)$.

Under these same conditions, Eq. 6 reduces to

$$P^*(\omega) = P(\omega) \qquad (7)$$

The required conditions for Eq. 7 to hold are again

$$P(\omega) = 0 \text{ for } |\omega| \geq \omega_0/2, \text{ and } F(\omega) = 1 \text{ for } |\omega| < \omega_0/2$$
$$F(\omega) = 0 \text{ for } |\omega| \geq \omega_0/2$$

Thus we have established our main claim and shown how a faithful replication of any frequency-limited function can be generated from samples.

What errors are produced if $P(\omega)$ is not frequency-limited? Figure 11 shows such a case. $P(\omega)$ is nonzero until ω equals $.9\omega_0$. The summation

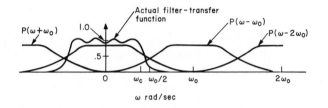

Fig. 11. Spectrum of $T \cdot Z(\omega)$ with function having a too wide frequency spectrum.

specified by Eq. 5 causes the tail ($P(\omega)$, $\omega_0/2 < \omega < \omega_0$) to add energy to $Z(\omega)$ in the frequency region $0 < \omega < \omega_0/2$. The tail is said to be folded around $\omega_0/2$, and hence the distortion is called foldover. Energy in $P(\omega)$ at frequencies ω appears in $P^*(\omega)$ at frequencies $\omega_0 - \omega$. This distortion is produced by the terms $P(\omega - \omega_0)$ and $P(\omega + \omega_0)$ in Eq. 5. If $P(\omega)$ contains even higher frequencies, distortions with frequency shifts of $2\omega_0 - \omega$ will be introduced by the $P(\omega - 2\omega_0)$ and $P(\omega + 2\omega_0)$ terms, and so forth.

In addition to foldover, errors are also introduced by the smoothing filter. The transfer function $F(\omega)$ is one term in Eq. 6. Realizable filters cannot achieve the ideal transfer function of unity for $|\omega| < \omega_0/2$ and zero for $|\omega| \geq \omega_0/2$. A typical function is sketched in Fig. 11. Two types of errors are caused. Departures of the amplitude from unity for $|\omega| < \omega_0/2$ distort $P^*(\omega)$ within the band of interest and produce in-band distortion. These distortions are typical of errors in other electronic equipment and are often measured in decibels of departure from unity or "flatness." Flatness within ± 1 dB is typical and easy to produce.

Departures of the amplitude from zero for $|\omega| \geq \omega_0/2$ add high-frequency energy to $P^*(\omega)$. For example, if $F(\omega_0) \neq 0$, a tone with a pitch equal to the sampling frequency will be heard. Gains as small as $1/100$ or $1/1000$ are not hard to achieve for $|\omega| \geq \omega_0/2$. In many cases the ear is not sensitive to the high frequencies and hence they are not objectionable. At a sampling rate of 30,000 Hz, all high-frequency distortions are at frequencies greater than 15,000 Hz and hence are almost inaudible.

One other limitation of realizable filters must be taken into account. They require a certain frequency band to change gain from unity to zero. In Fig. 11, the transition occurs between ω_c and $\omega_0/2$. Large distortions occur in this band; therefore it cannot contain useful components in $P^*(\omega)$. ω_c is effectively an upper limit for the usable frequency of $P^*(\omega)$, which is less than the theoretical maximum $\omega_0/2$. Typically $\omega_c = .8\omega_0/2$.

The spectrum $P^*(\omega)$ and hence $p^*(t)$ can be computed from Eq. 6 for any smoothing filter $F(\omega)$ and any $P(\omega)$. Thus the error $p(t) - p^*(t)$ can be computed. The calculation is complicated and is usually not worth carrying out. Instead, either a physical feeling for the error is obtained from a sketch such as Fig. 11 or bounds are computed for the error.

*Alternative Analysis of Sampling [2]

In sampling, we measure the amplitude of some voltage function $p(t)$, making the measurement R times per second. This sequence of R measurements per second constitutes the samples of the waveform $p(t)$.

The process of successive measurements of the amplitude of $p(t)$ can be carried out as shown in Fig. 12 by multiplying $p(t)$ by a succession of R equally spaced impulses per second, each with unit area. Thus the area (voltage times time) of each sample will be unity times the voltage

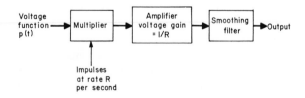

Fig. 12. Sampling-desampling process.

[2] Suggested by J. R. Pierce. This analysis is briefer than the preceding one and may be easier to understand.

of p(t) at the time of sampling. The number in the computer represents this area and is proportional to it.

We will disclose the consequences of such sampling by carrying out the multiplication in the frequency domain. The function p(t) will be represented by its Fourier transform

$$p(t) = \int_0^\infty A(f) \cos [2\pi ft - \varphi(f)] \, df$$

Here $A(f)$ is the amplitude of the voltage spectrum at the frequency f, and $\varphi(f)$ is the corresponding phase.

The voltage V_s of the R unit-area impulses per second is

$$V_s = R\left(1 + \sum_{n=1}^\infty 2 \cos 2\pi nRt\right)$$

In the process of multiplication, each spectral component of V_s interacts with the spectrum of p(t) to produce a new spectrum. The dc component of V_s produces simply p(t) multiplied by R. Each other spectral component of V_s produces a pair of *sidebands* lying about its frequency, $n\omega_0$ ($\omega_0 = 2\pi R$). To see this, note that by elementary trigonometry

$$(2R \cos 2\pi nRt) \cos [2\pi f - \varphi(f)]$$
$$= R\{\cos [2\pi(nR - f)t + \varphi(f)] + \cos [2\pi(nR + f)t - \varphi(f)]\}$$

Thus if we plot the amplitude voltage spectrum of the sampled wave, that is, of the samples, it appears as shown in Fig. 13. We see that if

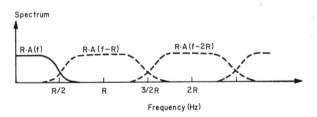

Fig. 13. Amplitude spectrum of sampled function.

p(t) contains frequencies higher than R/2, that is, if $A(f)$ is not zero for f larger than R/2, the sideband lying below the sampling rate R will fall partly within the frequency range from 0 to R/2. The higher frequencies of p(t) will have been *folded over* into the frequency range from 0 to R/2.

Let us return to Fig. 12, which illustrates the sampling process. Here we show the sampler (multiplier) followed by an amplifier of gain 1/R and a *smoothing filter* whose purpose is to remove frequencies above R/2 Hz.

Suppose first that p(t) contains no frequencies above R/2, and second that the smoothing filter has zero loss for all frequencies below R/2 and infinite loss for all frequencies above R/2. Then from the preceding analysis the output of the system should be exactly p(t).

That ideal performance can fail in two ways.

The voltage function p(t) may contain frequencies higher than R/2. In that case, folded-over frequencies will appear in the frequency range 0 to R/2, even though the smoothing filter is ideal.

The voltage function p(t) may contain no frequencies higher than R/2, but the smoothing filter may pass frequencies higher than R/2. In that case, some folded-over frequencies above R/2 Hz will pass through the smoothing filter.

In practice, we cannot make ideal smoothing filters. Rather, we count on using frequencies only up to some *cutoff frequency* fc, which is somewhat less than R/2, and try to make the smoothing filter loss increase rapidly enough with frequency above fc so that it passes little energy of frequency above R/2.

Bounding Sampling Errors

In most cases of practical interest, only four parameters describing the input spectrum $P(\omega)$ and the filter transfer function $F(\omega)$ need be considered to characterize the sampling errors adequately. These parameters are shown in Fig. 14.

The input spectrum (Fig. 14a) has been normalized to have unity maximum magnitude. The maximum magnitude for $\omega \geq \omega_0/2$ is m. The foldover error is characterized by the ratio m/1.0 or simply m. This number characterizes only the first foldover due to $P(\omega - \omega_0)$ and neglects higher folds on the assumption that $P(\omega)$ decreases rapidly at higher frequencies.

Allowable values for m are not well known. Values of 2 or 3 percent correspond to intermodulation distortions in much electronic equipment. If the frequency at which the m peak occurs is near $\omega_0/2$, large values can be tolerated because the folded energy will be generated at high frequencies (near $\omega_0/2$). By contrast, if the peak occurs near ω_0, the folded energy will appear at low frequencies and may be prominent and objectionable.

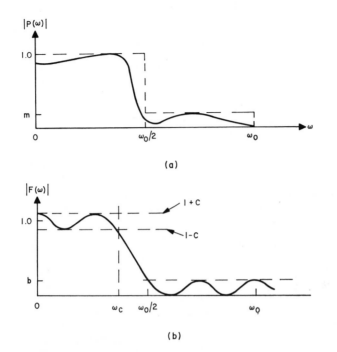

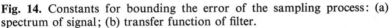

Fig. 14. Constants for bounding the error of the sampling process: (a) spectrum of signal; (b) transfer function of filter.

In trying to estimate whether the foldover of a given function $p(t)$ will be objectionable, a mental comparison of $p(t)$ with certain known waveforms may be useful. Figure 15 shows four waveforms—periodic impulses, a square wave, a triangular wave, and a sine wave.

The impulse function (Fig. 15a) has harmonics that do not decrease in amplitude; that is to say, the amplitude of the higher harmonics is the same as that of the fundamental. Such a function has prominent and usually objectionable foldover at any pitch. That behavior is typical of any function containing sharp pulses.

Figure 15b shows a square wave. Its harmonics decrease in amplitude as 1/frequency or 6 dB per octave. The square wave is usually good at low pitches (pitch less than 200 Hz for a sampling rate of 10,000 Hz). That behavior is typical for functions with sudden discontinuities.

Figure 15c shows a triangular wave. Its harmonics decrease as 1/(frequency)^2 or 12 dB per octave. It can usually be reproduced at pitches up to 1000 Hz with a 10,000-Hz sampling rate. It is typical of continuous functions with discontinuous derivatives.

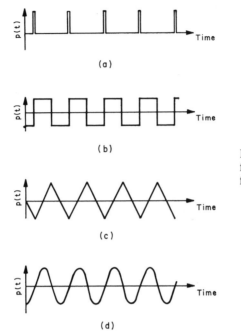

Fig. 15. Examples of p(t) functions with differing foldover.

To control the foldover of a very high-pitched function, p(t) may be formed from a sum of sine waves (Fig. 15d). In this way, foldover can be completely eliminated simply by having no components above $\omega_0/2$. The number of components must be changed at different pitches, which is an inconvenience.

Figure 14 shows the filter transfer function $F(\omega)$. It has been normalized to be approximately unity at low frequencies. The filter can be specified to deviate from unity gain by no more than c at low frequencies ($\omega \leq \omega_c$) and to have a maximum gain (leakage) b at high frequencies $\omega \geq \omega_0/2$. The sharpness of frequency cutoff is measured by $(\omega_0/2) - \omega_c$. The usable frequency range is from 0 to ω_c; hence ω_c should approach $\omega_0/2$.

Filter design and construction is a highly developed art. Typical values that are easy to obtain in specially designed filters are c = .1 (1 dB in-band deviation), b = 1/1000 (60 dB out-of-band attenuation) and $\omega_c = .8\omega_0/2$. General purpose filters or adjustable filters are not as good but are more convenient to buy and use. It is always desirable to have a flat in-band filter (c small). The importance of the out-of-band attenuation depends on the sampling rate. At low rates (10,000 Hz), out-of-band energy from 5000 Hz to 10,000 Hz must be carefully removed. At high rates (30,000 Hz), the out-of-band energy is above 15,000 Hz and hence is almost inaudible. Hence some sloppiness in the high-frequency filter performance is often tolerable. Note that such leniency does *not* apply to the high-frequency parts of P(ω). Here, high frequency energy folds and appears at low and prominent frequencies.

*Sample and Hold Analysis

The desampling process that we have analyzed assumed that impulses or very narrow pulses were put into the smoothing filter. In actual operation, wide pulses are usually used. A typical case is sketched in Fig. 3b, where the pulse width is 80 percent of the sampling time T. The gain of the desampling process is proportional to the pulse width, hence the advantage of wide pulses. However, a small distortion which we will now analyze is thus introduced in the spectrum of P*(ω). The distortion amounts to 4 dB in the worst case and is usually insignificant.

The holding process can be represented by introducing a filter between the impulse modulator and amplifier in Fig. 6. The impulse response of the filter h(t) is as shown in Fig. 16. Each impulse from the

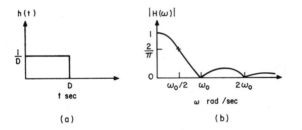

(a)   (b)

Fig. 16. Sample and hold circuit: (a) impulse response; (b) frequency function for D = T.

modulator is held for D seconds, thus producing a finite pulse. The transfer function H(ω) of this filter can be written

$$H(\omega) = \int_0^D \frac{1}{D} e^{-j\omega t}\, dt$$

The amplitude of the impulse response is taken as $1/D$ to normalize the low frequency gain of H(ω) to unity. Carrying out the integration, H(ω) is evaluated as

$$H(\omega) = e^{-j\omega D/2} \cdot \frac{\sin \omega D/2}{\omega D/2}$$

The maximum value of D is the full sampling time $D = T$. The magnitude of $H(\omega)$ for $D = T$ is plotted in Fig. 16b. The maximum distortion in $P^*(\omega)$ introduced by $H(\omega)$ occurs at $\omega = \omega_0/2$ and is $2/\pi$ or about 4 dB. The distortion decreases rapidly at lower frequencies. If $D = T/2$, the maximum distortion which again occurs at $\omega = \omega_0/2$ is only .9 or 1 dB.

*Analysis of Quantizing Errors

Quantizing errors are similar to noise in conventional electronic equipment. The two most important characteristics of noise are its magnitude and its frequency spectrum. We will derive an estimate of these for quantizing errors.

These errors are shown graphically in Fig. 17. A pressure wave p(t) is sketched in Fig. 17a with a much enlarged ordinate, so that the

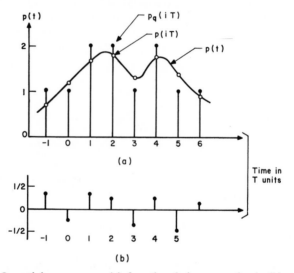

Fig. 17. Quantizing process: (a) function being quantized; (b) quantizing error.

quantizing levels 0, 1, and 2 are clear. The exact values p(iT) of p(t) at the sampling times are indicated by open circles. The analog-to-digital converter approximates these by the nearest quantizing level shown by the black dots $p_q(iT)$. The difference e_i where

$$e_i = p(iT) - p_q(iT) \tag{8}$$

is the quantizing error.

A sketch of the error is shown in Fig. 17b. The maximum magnitude of the error is $\frac{1}{2}$ because of the nature of the analog-to-digital converter. For this analysis, we will assume that each e_i is a random variable uniformly distributed over the range $-\frac{1}{2}$ to $+\frac{1}{2}$. We will also assume that e_i's at different sampling times are uncorrelated, that is, that $E\langle e_i e_j \rangle = 0$ for $i \neq j$. The notation $E\langle \ \rangle$ denotes expectation taken by an appropriate average.

These two assumptions are reasonable for $p(t)$ functions resulting from almost all sound waves. They are the only assumptions that lead to a simple estimate of the error. They neglect possible correlation between $p(t)$ and the error. This correlation has been noticed in one circumstance. During silent intervals, $p(t) = 0$, and e_i is constant. The spectral energy of the quantizing error will be entirely at zero frequency and thus inaudible. During nonsilent periods, the energy of e_i will be distributed across the audible spectrum. In this way the apparent noise seems to fluctuate with the signal, disappearing during silent intervals. This behavior contrasts with a normal tape recorder, in which background noise (tape hiss) is most prominent during silent intervals. For many listeners, the quantizing noise is less objectionable than an equivalent amount of tape hiss, because it tends to be masked by the signal when it is present.

We will now continue with the error analysis. Without quantizing errors the output of the sampling-desampling process shown in Fig. 6 can be written

$$p^*(t) = T \sum_{i=-\infty}^{\infty} p(iT)f(t - iT)$$

where $f(t)$ is the impulse response of the smoothing filter and is related to the filter frequency function by

$$f(t) = \frac{1}{2\pi} \int_{-\infty}^{+\infty} F(\omega)e^{j\omega t}\, d\omega$$

If the quantized samples $p_q(iT)$ are used as input to the impulse modulator, then the output $p_q^*(t)$ is

$$p_q^*(t) = T \sum_{i=-\infty}^{\infty} p_q(iT)f(t - iT)$$

The quantizing error $e_q(t)$ in the output is simply the difference $p^*(t) - p_q^*(t)$ and thus can be written

$$e_q(t) = T \sum_{i=-\infty}^{\infty} \{p(iT) - p_q(iT)\}f(t - iT) \tag{9}$$

which by Eq. 8 becomes

$$e_q(t) = T \sum_{i=-\infty}^{\infty} e_i f(t - iT)$$

The correlation function of $e_q(t)$ is by definition

$$\rho_q(\tau) = E\langle e_q(t)e_q(t + \tau)\rangle$$

Substituting Eq. 9 into the definition of $\rho_q(\tau)$, and taking advantage of the noncorrelated e_i's ($E\langle e_i e_j \rangle = 0$ for $i = j$), the correlation function simplifies to

$$\rho_q(\tau) = \overline{e^2} \cdot T \int_{-\infty}^{+\infty} f(t)f(t + \tau) \, dt$$

where $\overline{e^2}$ is the mean-square quantizing error

$$\overline{e^2} = E\langle e_i e_i \rangle$$

The energy spectrum of the quantizing error is by definition the transform of the correlation function

$$\Phi_q(\omega) = \frac{1}{2\pi} \int_{-\infty}^{+\infty} \rho_q(\tau)e^{-j\omega\tau} \, d\tau$$

and is

$$\Phi_q(\omega) = \frac{T}{2\pi} \overline{e^2}F(\omega)\overline{F(\omega)} \tag{10}$$

where $\overline{F(\omega)}$ indicates the conjugate of the frequency function of the filter.

For e_i uniformly distributed from $-\frac{1}{2}$ to $+\frac{1}{2}$

$$\overline{e^2} = \int_{-\frac{1}{2}}^{\frac{1}{2}} x^2 \, dx = \frac{1}{12}$$

For the ideal smoothing filter, $F(\omega) = 1$ for $|\omega| < \omega_0/2$ and $F(\omega) = 0$ for $|\omega| \geq \omega_0/2$, the energy in $\Phi_q(\omega)$ is uniformly distributed over the frequency band $-\omega_0/2$ to $\omega_0/2$. The mean-square quantizing error

$$\overline{e_q(t)^2} = \int_{-\infty}^{+\infty} \Phi_q(\omega) \, d\omega \tag{11}$$

$$= \int_{-\omega_0/2}^{\omega_0/2} \frac{T}{2\pi} \overline{e^2} \, d\omega$$

$$= \frac{\omega_0 T}{2\pi} \cdot \overline{e^2} = \overline{e^2} = \frac{1}{12} \tag{12}$$

The spectrum of the quantizing error can be computed from Eq. 10 and the mean-square error from Eq. 11 or Eq. 12. Thus we have completed our evaluation of quantizing error.

In order to compute the signal-to-quantizing-noise ratio, it is necessary to specify the signal. For example, if the signal is a sinusoid that occupies the entire range of quantizing levels (full-scale signal), it can be written

$$N/2 \sin \omega t$$

where N is the maximum number expressible with digits. The mean-square signal is $N^2/8$, and the ratio, rms signal to rms quantizing noise, is

$$\sqrt{(N^2/8)/(\tfrac{1}{12})} = \sqrt{(\tfrac{3}{2})}N$$

Earlier in the chapter we approximated this ratio as simply $N/.5$, which is reasonable in view of the assumptions made in the analysis.

In general, the rough considerations of quantizing errors discussed in the section on Sampling and Quantizing, are sufficient to control quantizing errors. A more precise analysis can be done, as outlined here, but is seldom worthwhile or necessary.

Digital-to-Analog and Analog-to-Digital Converters

Conversion between numbers in a computer and analog voltages is an essential step in sound processing. Happily, it is conceptually simple and practically easy to accomplish. A variety of commercial equipment can be purchased. Complete converters come as a unit, or they can be assembled from printed circuit cards sold by many computer companies. The commercial units and the assembly techniques are described in detail by their manufacturers; we will not reproduce this material, but simply explain the way they work and point out some of the errors and limitations.

Figure 18 shows the essential parts of a simple digital-to-analog converter. A binary number can be expanded as the sum of its digits times an appropriate power of 2. Thus, for example,

$$10011 = 1\cdot 2^4 + 0\cdot 2^3 + 0\cdot 2^2 + 1\cdot 2^1 + 1\cdot 2^0$$

At the input to the converter, the five digits that make up the number are represented by the voltages on five lines going to the switch controls $S_4 \ldots S_0$. A "1" is represented by a positive voltage and "0" by a

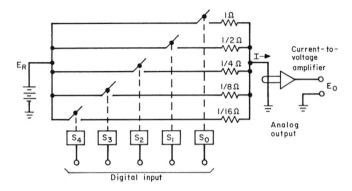

Fig. 18. Simple digital-to-analog converter.

negative voltage. The switch controls close their attached switch if they have a positive input and open it with a negative input.

The resistor network embodies the sum given above. The resistors are chosen to be inversely proportional to powers of 2. If F_i is a switching function that is 0 if S_i is open, and 1 if S_i is closed, then

$$I = E_R\{F_4 \cdot 16 + F_3 \cdot 8 + F_2 \cdot 4 + F_1 \cdot 2 + F_0 \cdot 1\}$$

Thus I is the analog equivalent of the digital input. The constant of proportionality is determined by the reference voltage E_R. The current-to-voltage amplifier generates an output voltage E_0 which is proportional to I.

In an actual converter, the switches would be transistors, the switch controls would be flip-flop registers, the current-to-voltage amplifier would be an operational amplifier, and the resistors would have values measured in thousands of ohms. Higher accuracy and more digits are obtained simply by adding more switches and resistors. Thus an actual converter is not much more complicated than the simple device we have described.

An analog-to-digital converter is more complicated. Most involve a digital-to-analog converter plus a feedback mechanism. The exact operation differs for different converters, but one widely used procedure is sketched in Fig. 19. The digital-to-analog converter that it contains can be made in the way that has been described. The complicated part is the programmer, which is effectively a small computer. A conversion is made in a sequence of steps. The analog voltage to be converted is applied to the analog input terminal. The programmer initially sets all the digits $S_4 \ldots S_0$ equal to zero. Digit S_4 is set to "1"

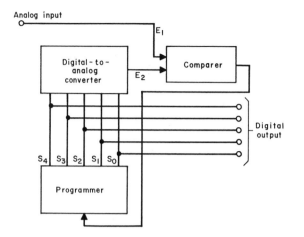

Fig. 19. Analog-to-digital converter.

as a trial. The resulting voltage E_2 from the digital-to-analog converter is compared with the input E_1. If $E_2 \leq E_1$, then S_4 remains "1." If $E_2 > E_1$, S_4 is reset to "0." The programmer carries out the same process with $S_3 \ldots S_0$. After five cycles involving five decisions from the comparer, $S_4 \ldots S_0$ is the digital equivalent of the analog input.

What are the limitations on speed and accuracy of converters? Usually speed is no problem with sound signals where sampling rates need be no faster than 40,000 Hz. The basic limitation on speed is the time for an electronic switch $S_0 - S_4$ to close, and for the transient voltages produced by the switching to disappear. Switches that settle in less than a microsecond are easy to build; hence sampling rates approaching 1 MHz are routine for digital-to-analog converters. Faster converters, up to 10 MHz, have been built using special circuits.

The analog-to-digital converter, as we have described it, is inherently n times slower than a digital-to-analog converter, where n is the number of digits. This limitation arises from the n sequential decisions involved in converting a single number, each decision requiring a digital-to-analog conversion. Thus, for example, a ten-digit converter with a 1-μs digital-to-analog part would have a maximum speed of 100 KHz.

One insidious error is inherent in the switching transients of a digital-to-analog converter. If all the switches do not operate at exactly the same speed, large errors will occur briefly during the change from certain digits to adjacent digits. For example, in going from 0111 to 1000 the analog output should change only one unit. However, all the digits change state. If the most significant digit is slightly faster than the other digits, the actual sequence will be 0111 1111 1000. The analog output resulting from the correct and erroneous sequence is shown in Fig. 20. It is clear that a large error is made momentarily. The error is difficult to observe because it depends on the signal, that is, it depends on transitions between particular levels, and it occurs very briefly.

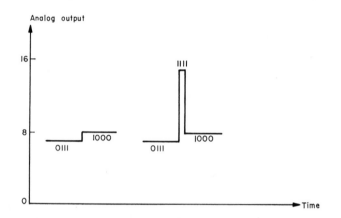

Fig. 20. Switching speed errors in digital-to-analog converter.

The error can be avoided in two ways. The switches can be carefully adjusted to have the same operating speed. A good commercial converter is usually satisfactory in this respect, whereas converters assembled from computer cards may need adjustment. Secondly, a

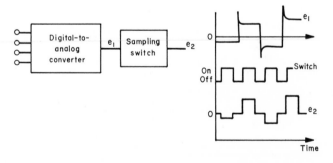

Fig. 21. Sampling switch to remove switching-speed errors.

sampling switch may be installed after the converter in order to gate out the error pulses. Figure 21 shows the connection and a graph of the operating waveforms.

Other errors in converters are fairly obvious. The quantizing error due to the finite number of digits has already been discussed. Fourteen is the maximum number of binary digits routinely available in commercial converters; 12 digits are often used for sound.

The resistors in the network attached to the switches must be accurate, particularly the small resistors. The tolerances can be maintained so that the maximum resistor error is much less than the least significant digit.

Other errors are essentially standard signal-to-noise problems inherent in all amplifiers and electronic equipment. With proper design, these can be kept insignificant in sound processing.

Smoothing-Filter Design

Filter design and construction is a highly developed science and art. Satisfactory smoothing filters can be either built or purchased. They can be of special design or of a standard type, or they can be variable with knob-controlled cutoff frequency. Consulting a filter expert is the best way to get just the right filter for a particular application. However, we will give instructions for building one smoothing filter that has been used for several years and is not too complicated.

The filter transfer function and circuit are shown on Fig. 22.[3] The version shown is intended for a 20-KHz sampling rate. It has less than 1 dB loss over the band 0 to 8 KHz. It has 60 dB or greater loss for all frequencies above 10 KHz. The filter is not corrected for phase and will distort the waveform of some signals. The phase change is less than that introduced by any tape recorder and is almost always inaudible.

In constructing the filter, the components should be adjusted to be within 1 percent of the values shown. An impedance bridge is used for the adjustment. Capacitors can be adjusted by obtaining one that is just under the desired value and adding a small capacitor in parallel. Inductors can be adjusted by obtaining an inductor just larger than the desired value and unwinding a few turns of wire. High-Q inductors of good quality should be used, for example, those with torodial or ferrite cores. The resistors are part of the source and load impedances and are usually not built into the filter.

[3] This filter was designed by F. C. Dunbar of the Bell Telephone Laboratories, Murray Hill, New Jersey.

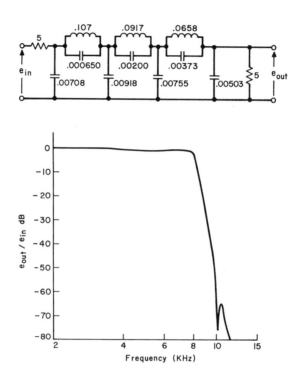

Fig. 22. Smoothing-filter circuit and transfer function. The filter has a dc gain of ½, which is not shown on the curve. Element values in KΩ, H, and μf.

Filters for other sampling rates can be built from this design by changing the values of the inductors and capacitors according to the equations

$$C' = C \cdot 20{,}000/f_s$$
$$L' = L \cdot 20{,}000/f_s$$

where C and L stand for the element values in the original design, C′ and L′ stand for the element values in the frequency-scaled design, and f_s is the new sampling rate. For example, a 10-KHz sampling rate is accommodated by doubling all inductors and capacitors.

As is shown on the circuit, the filter is designed to be driven by a 5-KΩ source impedance and to drive a 5-KΩ load. These impedances are not critical. The source impedance may vary from 2 KΩ to 5 KΩ, and the load impedance may vary from 5 KΩ to 100 KΩ without seriously changing the transfer function.

A filter can be constructed in a day with about $50 worth of parts. It is reasonably insensitive to the minor vicissitudes of a filter's life and has generally provided satisfactory performance.

Digital Data Storage and Retrieval for Sound

The nature of samples of sound waves requires some special consideration which will be developed here. A small amount of sound is represented by very many numbers. For example, one minute of sound sampled at 30 KHz produces 1,800,000 samples. When making either an analog-to-digital or a digital-to-analog conversion, the samples must be converted at an absolutely uniform rate! Variations in sampling rate are equivalent to flutter or wow in an ordinary tape recorder and are both audible and objectionable.

The number of samples is greater than the magnetic core memory of most computers; hence the samples must be stored in some bulk storage device. Fortunately since the samples are stored and retrieved in sequence, a digital magnetic tape is ideal.[4] However, most digital tapes do not store data continuously, but rather in groups called records. In order to send the samples to the converter at a uniform rate, a small core memory or buffer must be inserted between the tape and the converter.

A typical digital tape is ½-inch wide and 2400 ft long, and records data on six tracks at a density of 800 digits per inch. Thus 400 12-bit sound samples can be recorded on each inch. Allowing 10 percent of the tape for record gaps, the entire tape will hold 10^7 samples or 300 sec of sound sampled at 30,000 Hz. This is a practical if not large quantity.

The grouping of data into records is illustrated in Fig. 23. The record gaps provide space to start and stop the tape. The record and playback

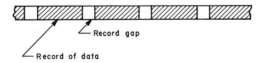

Fig. 23. Sample of digital magnetic tape showing record gaps.

heads are initially positioned at the first record gap. The tape is started, one record of data is transmitted, and the tape is stopped with the

---

[4] Magnetic disk recording is also possible but has little advantage over tape since the sound samples are in such an orderly sequence.

record-playback heads at the next record gap. The tape is kept in motion through an entire record, since reading is unreliable during starting and stopping.

The minimum length of the record gap is determined by the tape speed and the rapidity with which it is started and stopped. A ¾-inch gap and starting and stopping times of 3 to 5 msec are typical.

The maximum data rate from the tape is simply the tape speed times the density of samples per inch. Thus typical speeds ranging from 60 inches per second to 150 inches per second and a density of 400 samples per inch correspond to maximum data rates of 24,000 Hz to 60,000 Hz. Achievable rates are slightly less than these maxima because of time spent starting and stopping.

The control mechanism to start and stop a digital tape recorder, to store the digital samples, and to transmit them to a converter at a uniform rate is unfortunately complicated and expensive. A simple schematic diagram is shown in Fig. 24. The digital tape transmits a

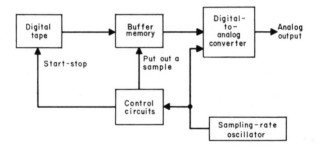

Fig. 24. Digital-tape control for sound.

record of data to the buffer memory. The buffer is a core memory controlled so that the output samples will be in the same sequence as were the samples put into it. It has sufficient flexibility so that its output and input can be interleaved in any order. The sampling rate is, and should be, controlled by a single oscillator, which can easily be set to any desired sampling rate. Each cycle from the oscillator causes the buffer to deliver another sample to the converter and the converter to output the sample. The control circuits keep track of the number of samples in the buffer memory and start the tape recorder before it is empty.

The size of the buffer memory is determined by the record length of the tape data. If any sampling rate from zero up to nearly the tape data rate is to be accommodated, then a buffer longer than one record is necessary. A length equal to two records simplifies the control circuits.

The design must take consideration of these facts: larger buffers cost more, longer records yield higher maximum rates because of fewer record gaps, the tape must be started soon enough to avoid emptying the buffer at the highest sampling rate, the buffer must be large enough never to overfill at the lowest sampling rate. A design is a proper compromise between these factors. Although we have only discussed a digital-to-analog conversion system, the analog-to-digital process requires the same buffer and works in a basically similar manner.

The digital tape controller that we have described is rather expensive and complicated to build. Often the computer itself makes a more attractive tape controller. A schematic diagram is shown in Fig. 25.

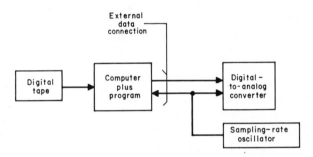

Fig. 25. Computer as tape control for sound.

In order to function in this way, the computer must have an external data connection which will deliver samples to a converter under the control of an *external* oscillator. Most recent computers can be obtained with this feature. The digital tape transport can be one normally associated with the computer, the computer's core memory serves as buffer, and functions of the control circuits are accomplished by a suitable program. Thus the same machine that synthesizes or analyzes the sound can also communicate directly in sound with the external world.

Fundamental Programming Problems for Sound Synthesis

In the preceding material we have described a powerful and flexible technology for sound processing by computer. The remaining ingredient is the computer programs that activate this technology; but that is a large ingredient. Most of the rest of this book can be considered as descriptions of some of these programs. Sound processing can be divided into sound analysis and sound synthesis. So far, no universal programs for analysis have been developed. Rather, many different programs have been written for particular tasks. For synthesis, one program, which developed through five stages, Music I–Music V, has proved generally useful. Hence we will present here the fundamental considerations that led to Music V, and in the next chapters details intended to teach a user of Music V. However, the material should be of value not only to users of Music V, but to anyone writing a sound-synthesis program.

The two fundamental problems in sound synthesis are (1) the vast amount of data needed to specify a pressure function—hence the necessity of a very fast and efficient computer program—and (2) the need for a simple, powerful language in which to describe a complex sequence of sounds. Our solution to these problems involves three principles: (1) *stored functions* to speed computation, (2) *unit-generator* building blocks for sound-synthesizing instruments to provide great flexibility, and (3) the *note concept* for describing sound sequences. Let us next consider sound synthesis from the computer's and the composer's standpoints to see the importance of these principles.

To specify a pressure function at a sampling rate of 30 KHz, one number is needed every 33 μsec. That speed strains even the fastest computers. A useful measure of computation is the time scale, which is defined as

$$\text{Time scale} \equiv \frac{\text{time to compute samples of a sound}}{\text{duration of the sound}}$$

Various possibilities exist at various time scales. If the time scale is equal to 1 or less, a digital-to-analog converter can be attached directly to the computer and sound can be synthesized in real time. This allows improvising on the computer, hearing the sound as one pushes the computer keys in the same way that one hears sound from a piano. Fast current computers add two numbers in about 3 μsec and multiply two numbers in about 30 μsec. Hence the computations for each sample for real-time synthesis must be few indeed. However, real-time synthesis is a powerful way of adjusting sound parameters to achieve a particular timbre or effect. In addition, it allows the computer to be used as a performing instrument. Hence it is an important objective.

Time scales greater than 1 necessitate recording the samples on a digital magnetic tape, rewinding the tape, and playing the tape through the converter. A delay equal to or greater than the sound duration is inherent in the process. Time scales from 1 to 50 are eminently usable. At 50, a delay of an hour is needed to compute one minute of sound.

An hour seems long if you personally are waiting for the computer; it is nothing if you are at home sleeping while the night shift runs the problem. At a scale of 50, 1600 µsec are available to compute each sample. Fifty multiplications or several hundred additions can be carried out in that time. Although much can be done, that number of computations does not represent a copious supply, and it must be used effectively.

Time scales from 50 to 1000 become so time consuming and expensive that even the most reckless experimenter pauses to consider whether the value of his sounds justifies the time and money. At a scale of 1000, 20 minutes of computer time are needed for each second of sound. It must be a remarkable second to make this effort seem worth while.

One way of speeding the effective computation is to store samples in the computer memory, when possible, and to read these samples from memory rather than recompute them. Reading from memory is rapid. The process works only for samples or factors of samples that are repetitive. Fortunately, many sounds have highly repetitive components. For example, an oscillator repeats the same waveform each cycle. The shape of a cycle's wave may be very complicated, but once it is computed and stored, it can be read out as rapidly as any simple function. Many other factors can be reduced to repetitive stored functions.

The cost of *stored functions* is memory space. In Music V a typical function is stored as 512 samples, and the largest part of the memory is used for storing functions. The cost is more than justified by the time saved.

We have considered sound synthesis from the position of the computer and it has led us to stored functions. Now let us look from the composer's standpoint. He would like to have a very powerful and flexible language in which he can specify any sequence of sounds. At the same time he would like a very simple language in which much can be said in a few words, that is, one in which much sound can be described with little work. The most powerful and universal possibility would be to write each of the millions of samples of the pressure wave directly. This is unthinkable. At the other extreme, the computer could operate like a piano, producing one and only one sound each time one of 88 numbers was inserted. This would be an expensive way to build a piano. The *unit-generator* building blocks make it possible for the composer to have the best of both of these extremes.

With unit generators the composer can construct, with a simple procedure, his own sound-synthesizing program. In Music V it is called the orchestra, and it contains a number of different subprograms called instruments. The unit generators perform functions that experience has shown to be useful. For example, there are oscillators, adders, noise generators, and attack generators. Many unit generators perform conceptually similar functions to standard electronic equipment used for electronic sound synthesis.

In a given instrument the composer can connect as many or as few unit generators together as he desires. Thus he can literally take any position he chooses between the impossible freedom of writing individual pressure-function samples and the straightjacket of the computer piano. In this way, in unit-generator building blocks, we have given the composer almost ultimate flexibility to choose the environment in which to work. The price is the work he must do in constructing the instruments in his orchestra. However, the language with which the unit generators are assembled is so elegant that this cost is insignificant.

The final principle for specifying sound sequences is the *note concept*. Sound exists as a continuous function of time starting at the beginning of a piece and extending to the end. We have chosen, for practical reasons, to chop this continuous sound into discrete pieces, called notes, each of which has a starting time and a duration time. This division is admittedly a restriction on the generality of sound synthesis, but one we are not brave enough to avoid. Needless to add, notes have been around for some time.

The note concept interacts with the instrument in a straightforward way. The instruments are designed to "play" notes. At the starting time of each note, a set of instructions is given to the instrument, and it is turned on for the duration of the note. No further information is given to the instrument during the course of the note; the complexity of the instrument determines the complexity of the sound of the note.

The instructions for the instrument for each note are written on a score by the composer (or by the composer's program if he wishes to delegate this task to the computer). Hence, the complexity and length of the instructions, multiplied by the number of notes, determines the amount of work the composer must do. In general, complicated instruments require more instructions, but they may be able to play longer and more interesting notes. Within the limitations of these conflicting factors, the composer must create an environment in which he is willing to work.

The note concept also includes the idea of *voices*, which have their usual musical meaning. In Music V instruments can play any number of notes at the same time. The program adds all voices and puts out the combined sound. The addition is simple for the computer. Furthermore, it automatically synchronizes all voices. Each note has a starting time. The computer arranges all notes in a composition into the proper time sequence, and thus the composer can write the score in any order he chooses. In this way the tyranny of time, which so harasses the performing musician, is almost completely eliminated by the computer.

The fundamentals of stored functions, unit generators, and notes have been given general consideration here. Details of their use in the Music V program appear frequently in the following chapters.

Overview of Sound-Synthesis Program—Music V

Next we discuss the over-all operation of the Music V program, both as an example of a sound-synthesis program and as an introduction to the more detailed material that follows.

An outline of the program is shown in Fig. 26. Programs change; the description given here is the program as it was created in 1967–1968.

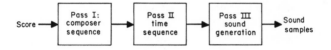

Fig. 26. Outline of sound-synthesis program.

It ran on a General Electric 635 computer but was programmed almost entirely in FØRTRAN IV to simplify its transposition to other machines. For concreteness, we will speak of this specific historical program. However, most of what we shall say applies to other computers. Also, the basic program has been modified in many ways for special purposes, such as adding another input section to accommodate graphical scores. These will be described later.

The composer speaks to the computer through a score that contains not only the notes to be played but also descriptions of the instruments on which they will be played.

The orchestra description specifies each instrument in the orchestra in terms of the type of each unit generator in it and how the unit generators are interconnected or related. Types of unit generators—oscillators, adders, random sources—are straightforward. Many interconnections are possible. For example, the outputs of two oscillators can be added to produce a more complex tone, or one oscillator can control the frequency of a second oscillator to produce a vibrato.

Inherent in the description of each instrument are the input parameters needed to run it. For example, if the instrument is to play notes of differing pitches, one input parameter must specify pitch. If vibrato is to have a controllable rate, a parameter must specify this rate. These parameters must eventually be supplied by the score.

Different instruments must be uniquely designated. This is done simply by numbering them. Thus the program will have instruments 1, 2, 3, and so forth, and the score will request a note to be played by an instrument number.

The sound synthesis is divided into three sections for both conceptual and computational reasons. Pass I reads the score written by the composer. It may contain *note cards* requesting the synthesis of a specific note, instruction cards which cause Pass I to produce note cards, and cards to set functions and parameters in Passes I, II, and III. Each note card must contain an instrument number, the starting time of the note, and the duration of the note. All other quantities on the card depend entirely on what input parameters the composer has specified in his instrument.

If notes are to be played, the score must also contain cards defining instruments. These also contain the time at which the instrument is to be defined. It is possible to redefine an instrument part way through the composition, thus changing the timbre.

Pass I reads and processes the score in the sequence in which the composer has written it. Note cards written by the composer are simply sent directly to Pass II. Instruction cards may cause subroutines in Pass I to generate or compose note cards which are then sent to Pass II. Thus, most of the composing power of the program resides in Pass I.

The note cards written by either the composer or Pass I can be written in any time sequence; this gives great flexibility. Furthermore, notes for different voices can be intermixed in any order.

In Pass II all note cards are sorted into increasing time sequence to prepare for sound generation. Parameters on the note cards may be modified by FØRTRAN subroutines. For example, the frequency ratio between two voices at a given time can conveniently be adjusted because all voices are in proper time sequence. Metronome markings to accelerate or retard the time scale are convenient to apply in Pass II. However, once the notes are ordered for time, new notes cannot be added without destroying the ordering. Hence, new note cards cannot be generated in Pass II.

Pass III reads the note cards after they have been time ordered by Pass II. At the beginning of each note, the parameters from the note card are inserted into the appropriate instrument and the instrument is turned on for the duration of the note.

To summarize, the complete program with three passes, stored functions, unit generators, and instruments was evolved over several years. It is not a unique way of synthesizing sound samples; other equivalent programs could be written. However, it does provide great speed and great flexibility by the careful use of a general compiling language (FØRTRAN) plus certain machine language subroutines.

Annotated References by Subject

Sound in General
P. M. Morse, *Vibration and Sound* (McGraw-Hill, New York, 1948). A mathematical, technical book written from the physicist's standpoint.

C. A. Taylor, *The Physics of Musical Sounds* (English Underwriters Press, London, 1965). A less technical book than Morse's; still from the physicist's standpoint.

Sampling, Foldover Errors, etc.
J. R. Ragazzini and G. F. Franklin, *Sampled-Data Control Systems* (McGraw-Hill, New York, 1958). The first chapters treat sampling and desampling in general and are not limited to control systems.

Quantizing Errors
W. R. Bennett, "Spectra of Quantized Signals," *Bell Sys. Tech. J. 27*, 446 (1948) The fundamental analysis of quantizing errors.

Analog-Digital Conversion
B. W. Stephenson, *Analog-Digital Conversion Handbook* (Digital Equipment Corporation, Maynard, Mass., 1964). A combined catalog and instruction book for making digital circuits from plug-in components (manufactured by the Digital Equipment Corp.).

Note: Several companies manufacture analog-digital conversion equipment. These may change from year to year. Currently, the Texas Instrument Company and the Raytheon Company make satisfactory apparatus for sound processing.

Filter Design
M. E. Van Valkenburg, *Introduction to Modern Network Synthesis* (John Wiley & Sons, New York, 1960). A good presentation of some of the many details of network synthesis from the standpoint of the electrical engineer.

Digital Data Storage and Retrieval
E. E. David, Jr., M. V. Mathews, and H. S. McDonald, "Description and Results of Experiments with Speech Using Digital Computer Simulation," *Proceedings of 1958 National Electronics Conference*, pp. 766–775.

E. E. David, Jr., M. V. Mathews, and H. S. McDonald, "A High-Speed Data Translator for Computer Simulation of Speech and Television Devices," *Proceedings of I.R.E. Western Joint Computer Conference*, pp. 354–357 (1959).

These articles describe some of the first equipment for computer sound processing. The equipment is obsolete, but the principles are valid and important.

Fundamental Programming Problem
M. V. Mathews, "An Acoustic Compiler for Music and Psychological Stimuli," *Bell Sys. Tech. J. 40*, 677–694 (May 1961).

M. V. Mathews, "The Digital Computer as a Musical Instrument," *Science 142,* 553–557 (November 1963).

J. R. Pierce, M. V. Mathews, and J. C. Risset, "Further Experiments on the Use of the Computer in Connection with Music," *Gravesaner Blätter,* No. 27/28, 92–97 (November 1965).

These are the original papers that trace the development of the current sound-synthesizing program.

Problems for Chapter 1

Numerical Representations of Functions of Time

1. Sketch pressure functions that

(a) Are periodic with a period of 1 millisecond (msec)

(b) Have a fundamental pitch of 600 Hz

(c) Have energy only at 500 Hz

(d) Have energy at 500 Hz and 750 Hz (what is the period of this function?)

(e) Have energy only at zero frequency

(f) Have no perceivable periodicity

2. On the same sheet of paper, draw three functions that are periodic with periods of (a) 10 msec, (b) 5 msec, and (c) 1 msec. What are the pitches of these functions?

3. Desample the following sequences of numbers. Draw a graph of the pulses from a sample-and-hold desampling circuit. Assume a 50-percent duty factor for the pulses. Pass a smooth waveform through the pulses in a manner in which you imagine a smoothing filter would operate

(a) 0, 3, 5, 7, 10, 13, 15, 17, 20, 22, 25, 28, 30, 24, 20, 15, 10, 6, 0, -4, -7, -9, -10, -10, -9, -7, 0

(b) 0, 7, 10, 7, 0, -7, -10, -7, 0

(c) 10, -10, 10, -10, 10, -10, 10, -10 (for case c draw at least two possible smooth waveforms; which one would be passed by a low-pass filter having a cutoff frequency appropriate to the sampling rate?)

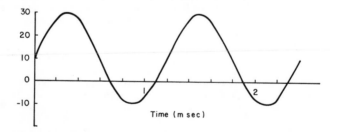

4. Sample and quantize 2 msec of the waveform shown above at a sampling rate of

(a) 1000 Hz   (b) 2000 Hz   (c) 5000 Hz

(d) Which sampling rate seems "visually" sufficient to characterize the waveform?

(e) Assume the wave has energy at only two frequencies; what are these frequencies?

(f) What is the minimum faithful sampling rate according to the sampling theorem?

(g) What is the period and pitch of the wave?

Sampling

5. A waveform p(t) where

$$
\begin{aligned}
p(t) = {} & 100 \text{ sine } (2\pi \cdot 2100 \cdot t) + 50 \text{ sine } (2\pi \cdot 4200 \cdot t) \\
& + 33 \text{ sine } (2\pi \cdot 6300 \cdot t) + 25 \text{ sine } (2\pi \cdot 8400 \cdot t) \\
& + 20 \text{ sine } (2\pi \cdot 10{,}500 \cdot t) + 17 \text{ sine } (2\pi \cdot 12{,}600 \cdot t) \\
& + 14 \text{ sine } (2\pi \cdot 14{,}700 \cdot t) + 12 \text{ sine } (2\pi \cdot 16{,}800 \cdot t) \\
& + 11 \text{ sine } (2\pi \cdot 18{,}900 \cdot t) + 10 \text{ sine } (2\pi \cdot 21{,}000 \cdot t)
\end{aligned}
$$

is subjected to a sampling and desampling process as shown in Fig. 6. The sampling rate is 19 kHz. The desampled output is p*(t).

(a) What is the highest frequency component that can be faithfully reproduced in p*(t) at this sampling rate? Call this component and all lower components the desired components. Give the amplitudes and frequencies of components of p*(t) with

(b) no smoothing filter

(c) a filter with the frequency function

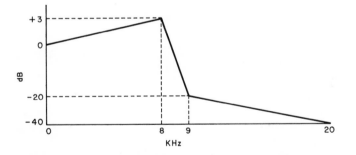

(d) Also give the amplitudes and frequencies of the components of p(t).

(e) What is the lowest frequency component in p(t)? What is p(t)'s period? What is its pitch?

(f) What is the lowest frequency component in p*(t) with no smoothing filter? What is p*(t)'s period?

(g) How much are the desired components in p*(t) changed by the filter? Which desired component is most changed?

(h) Which distortion components in the "range of perception" (0–15 kHz) are reduced by the filter? Which are relatively unaffected?

(i) What distortion components that are folded about 38 kHz fall in the range of perception?

(j) With no filter, what is the maximum frequency that can be reproduced without causing a distortion component in the range of perception?

(k) With the filter, what is the maximum frequency that can be reproduced without causing a distortion component in the range of perception (assume filter has infinite attenuation for frequencies greater than 9 kHz)?

6. Samples at a 20-kHz rate are computed for the waveform

$$f(t) = \text{sine}\left[2\pi \cdot \left(\frac{60{,}000 \cdot t}{30}\right) \cdot t\right]$$

$$+ \text{sine}\left[2\pi \cdot \left(\frac{30{,}000(20 - t)}{30}\right) \cdot t\right]$$

The sound is desampled with an impulse desampler and no filter. Describe the amplitudes and frequencies of the components that fall within the range of perception (0 to 15 kHz); t goes from 0 to 30 sec.

Analog-Digital Conversion

7. Calculate the tolerance on the resistors in the digital-to-analog converter shown in Fig. 18 so that the maximum error due to any one resistor is $\frac{1}{10}$ of one quantizing level. Give tolerance in terms of both absolute accuracy and percent accuracy. Which resistor must have the best percent accuracy?

Smoothing Filter Design

8. Frequency scale the filter shown in Fig. 22 so that the cutoff frequency is

(a) 15 kHz corresponding to a sampling frequency of 30 kHz;
(b) 3 kHz corresponding to a sampling frequency of 6 kHz.

Digital Data Storage and Retrieval

9. Suppose that you have a digital tape with data recorded at 400 samples per inch and a tape speed of 100 inches per second. The record gaps are 1 inch long; the tape takes 6 msec to stop after reading the last sample in a record and 10 msec to start (time from start signal to reading of first sample in record).

(a) Calculate the maximum data rate for record lengths of 100, 500, 2500, and 10,000 samples.

(b) Calculate the minimum buffer size for each record length to accommodate data rates for 0 up to the maximum.

For safety, design the control so the buffer will never have less than 50 samples and will always have 50 or more empty cells.

(c) At what number of samples in the buffer should the tape start signal be given?

2 A Sequence of Tutorial Examples of Sound Generation

Introduction

This chapter is intended to provide a training course in the use of Music V by discussing a series of examples ranging from simple to complex sound synthesis. It is written from the point of view of the user of Music V. Details of operation of the programs will be suppressed as much as possible. These can be found in Chapter 3. Because the programs will not be described here, many of the conventions of the computer score will seem arbitrary and must be temporarily accepted on faith.

For concreteness we will also arbitrarily assume values for certain parameters of the program, for example, a sampling rate of $R = 20,000$ Hz. Other parameters will be introduced as required. For the student's benefit, the parameters of the training orchestra are listed at the beginning of the problems for Chapter 2.

The material assumes that the student has a working knowledge of FØRTRAN programming. The programming examples will be written in FØRTRAN IV. It is also assumed that the student understands the general functioning of a computer—arithmetic, memory, input–output, and program. If necessary, these skills can be learned from books cited in the references at the end of Chapter 2.

This chapter is intended as training material and not as a reference manual for Music V. Reference material is organized and presented in Chapter 3.

The Simplest Orchestra

By way of introduction, an elementary orchestra and score are shown in Fig. 27. We shall start by describing the material and then explain the details of its operation. Figure 27a shows the conventional score of the few notes that will be synthesized. Figure 27b shows the block diagram of the simulated instrument that will play the score. It consists solely of an oscillator and an output box. The oscillator has two inputs; the amplitude of the output equals P5; the frequency is proportional to P6. The waveform of the oscillation is determined by stored function F2, which is sketched in Fig. 27c.

The records in the computer score, Fig. 27d have been numbered for reference in this discussion. Each record has a sequence of entries designated P1, P2, P3, etc. In the training orchestra, up to 30 entries (P1–P30) may be used. The entries are separated either by blank spaces or by a comma. Each record is terminated by a semicolon. A record may extend over several lines; conversely, several records may be put on one line.

Records 1 through 4 define, for the computer, the instrument shown in Fig. 27b. INS 0 1; says that, at time 0 in the composition, instrument 1 will be defined. ØSC P5 P6 B2 F2 P30 ; says that the first unit generator in the instrument will be an oscillator, will have inputs P5 and P6, will use function F2 for its waveform, will store its output in I–Ø block B2, and will use P30 for temporary storage (which we will discuss later). ØUT B2 B1; says to take the samples in I–Ø block B2 and add them to the contents of block B1 in preparation for outputting these samples. END; terminates the instrument definition.

Record 5 defines the function F2 (Fig. 27c) and causes it to be generated and stored in the computer memory assigned to F2.

Notes 1 through 11 in the score are generated by records 6 through 16, respectively. In each of the records P1 (NØT) says the purpose of the record is to play a note. P2 gives the starting time of the note measured in seconds from the beginning of the composition. P3 (1) gives the instrument number on which the note will be played. P4 gives the duration of the note in seconds. Durations of staccato notes are written to produce more silence between successive notes than the corresponding silence for the legato notes. P5 gives the amplitude of the note as required by the instrument. In the training orchestra, amplitude can vary over the range 0 to 2047. Amplitudes are varied to

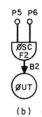

(a)

(b)

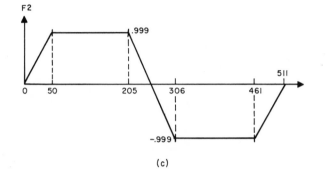

(c)

```
 1  INS 0 1 ;
 2  ØSC P5 P6 B2 F2 P30 ;
 3  ØUT B2 B1 ;
 4  END ;
 5  GEN 0 1 2 0 0 .999 50 .999 205 −.999 306 −.999 461 0 511 ;
 6  NØT 0 1 .50 125 8.45 ;
 7  NØT .75 1 .17 250 8.45 ;
 8  NØT 1.00 1 .50 500 8.45 ;
 9  NØT 1.75 1 .17 1000 8.93 ;
10  NØT 2.00 1 .95 2000 10.04 ;
11  NØT 3.00 1 .95 1000 8.45 ;
12  NØT 4.00 1 .50 500 8.93 ;
13  NØT 4.75 1 .17 500 8.93 ;
14  NØT 5.00 1 .50 700 8.93 ;
15  NØT 5.75 1 .17 1000 13.39 ;
16  NØT 6.00 1 1.95 2000 12.65 ;
17  TER 8.00 ;
```

(d)

Fig. 27. Elementary orchestra and score: (a) conventional score; (b) instrument block diagram; (c) waveform; (d) computer score.

correspond to the dynamic markings on the conventional score. P6 equals .02555 times the frequency of the note in cycles per second (hertz). The proportionality constant .02555 will be explained below. Record 17 terminates the composition at 8 sec.

Simple Unit Generators to Output, Add, and Multiply

Having introduced a simple orchestra and score from the user's standpoint, we will now describe in more detail the operation of a few simple unit generators. Although they are simple, these are the most frequently used building blocks for all instruments.

As we showed in Chapter 1, the acoustic output wave is produced by passing a sequence of numbers (samples) $s_0, s_1, \ldots, s_i$ through a digital-to-analog converter and driving a loudspeaker with the analog voltage from the converter. The first sample s_0 is the amplitude of the acoustic wave at the beginning of the composition at $t = 0$, where t is time. The second sample s_1 is the amplitude one sampling time later. We shall assume a sampling rate of 20,000 Hz for the training orchestra; hence s_1 is put out at $t = 1/20,000$ sec. $s_{40,000}$ is the amplitude at $t = 2$ sec. It is quite possible, though seldom useful, to specify the sample that controls the amplitude of the acoustic output at any $1/20,000$ sec throughout the entire composition.

The purpose of the portions of the Music V program called "instruments" is to calculate all the s_i samples. For example, if a note is to be played from 3 sec to 4 sec in the composition, samples $s_{60,000}$ through $s_{80,000}$ must be computed. The nature of $s_{60,000}$ through $s_{80,000}$ determines the characteristics of the sound—its pitch, loudness, timbre, everything. The nature of the samples is, in turn, determined by the particular unit generators that are put together to form the instrument and by the numbers on the data records that control these generators.

A problem that must be solved by Music V is to keep track of time so as to "turn on" a given instrument program at the sample at which its note should begin, and to "turn off" the instrument at the sample at which its note should end. The starting sample is computed simply by multiplying the starting time of the note given in P2 by the sampling rate. The terminating time is P2 plus the duration P4, and the terminating sample number is the sampling rate times the terminating time. Because of the universal necessity for this control of time, P2 and P4 must always be used for starting time and duration in all records which specify notes.

A second problem facing Music V is to combine the numbers from all instruments that are playing simultaneously at a given time. The digital-to-analog conversion process demands that the samples be output in sequence, s_1 followed by s_2, followed by s_3, and so forth. Thus the contribution of all instruments to a sample must be computed simultaneously. A way to accomplish this end, which has been used in earlier programs, is to calculate one number from each active instrument, combine these numbers (by addition), output the sample, and then proceed to the next sample. Music V operates in essentially this way, but for additional efficiency it calculates a block of numbers from each instrument instead of a single number. These blocks, called I-Ø blocks, are one of the fundamental data storage units in the program.

I-Ø Blocks

I-Ø blocks are short for unit generator input–output blocks. They can be used as storage locations for either inputs or outputs for unit generators, hence the designation input–output blocks. Blocks are designated B1 through B10 in the training orchestra. Block B1 has the special function of storing the numbers that will be sent to the digital-to-analog converter. All other blocks are equivalent in mono. (In stereo, blocks B1 and B2 are both reserved for output.)

The size of the block is a parameter of the orchestra. In the training orchestra, it has been set at 512. The maximum size of numbers in the I-Ø blocks is another program parameter. In the training orchestra it has been set at ± 2047 which is appropriate for a 12-bit digital-to-analog converter.

AD2 Generator

The simplest generator is the two–input adder, AD2. Its function is to combine two numbers by addition. It has two inputs and one output as shown in Fig. 28a. The equation of operation is

$$\emptyset_i = I1_i + I2_i$$

where I1 and I2 are the two inputs, Ø is the output, and i is the index of samples that starts at 0 at time $t = 0$. We must quickly add that this equation is computed only for those samples during which the instrument with AD2 is playing a note.

In the score, AD2 is put in an instrument by a statement such as

AD2 B2 B4 B3 ;

This example says: take the numbers stored in block B2, add them to those stored in block B4, and put the sum in block B3. The relation

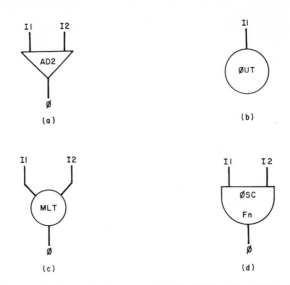

Fig. 28. Four simple unit generators: (a) AD2; (b) ØUT; (c) MLT; (d) ØSC.

between sample index i and the numbers in a given block at a given time need not worry the user; it is treated automatically by the program.

AD3 and AD4 also exist and form a sum of three and four inputs, respectively. The score statement evoking AD4 would be

    AD4 B2 B3 B4 B5 B6 ;

where B2 through B5 are inputs and B6 the output.

ØUT Generator

The ØUT generator takes the numbers from an instrument and places them in the special I-Ø block B1 for subsequent outputting through the digital-to-analog converter. ØUT also combines the numbers with any other instrument simultaneously being played. ØUT is diagrammed in Fig. 28b. It is shown with one input. The output to B1 is not shown; it always goes to this block. The equation of operation is in FØRTRAN-like notation

$$\text{Acoustic output}_i = \text{acoustic output}_i + \text{I1}_i$$

This equation says: I1 is added to anything previously in the acoustic output block; by this simple means any number of instruments may be combined. The operation of addition is perfectly equivalent to the way in which sound waves of several real instruments combine in the air.

In the score ØUT is evoked by a statement such as

ØUT B2 B1;

where B2 is the block containing the input, and B1 is the special block for acoustic output.

MLT Generator

The MLT generator multiplies two numbers together in a manner exactly analogous to the addition done by AD2. It is diagrammed in Fig. 28c. The equation of operation is

$$\emptyset_i = I1_i \cdot I2_i$$

where I1 and I2 are the two inputs and Ø is the output. In the score

MLT B2 B3 B4 ;

associates I1 with B2, I2 with B3, and Ø with B4. In general, the order of listing generator descriptions on the score is: inputs, outputs, special parameters.

ØSC Generator[1]

By far the most important generator is the oscillator ØSC. It is the most frequently used and the most difficult to understand of the simple generators. Its importance is based on the prominence of oscillations in musical sounds and on its nature as a *source* of numbers. The generators previously described modify or output numbers that have been created elsewhere; ØSC is one of the few units that actually produce numbers.

The diagram of ØSC is presented in Fig. 28d. As will be shown, three quantities determine the output Ø: I1 controls the amplitude of the oscillation; I2 controls the frequency; and F_n, a stored function, is the waveform. F_n is exactly one cycle of the ØSC output; the purpose of the ØSC can be looked upon as repeating F_n at the desired frequency and amplitude.

F_n may be thought of as a continuous function of time, but in the computer it must be represented by a block of samples. In the training orchestra each function is represented by 512 samples. Figure 29 shows an example of a stored function F3. The waveform is a square wave with slightly slanted sides. The 512 points, $F3(k)\ k = 0\ldots511$, are

---

[1] Also see Chapter 3, Section 6, for a basic discussion of ØSC.

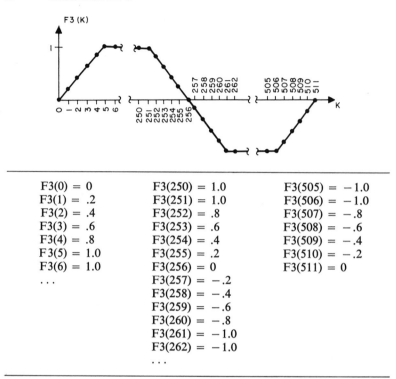

F3(0) = 0	F3(250) = 1.0	F3(505) = −1.0
F3(1) = .2	F3(251) = 1.0	F3(506) = −1.0
F3(2) = .4	F3(252) = .8	F3(507) = −.8
F3(3) = .6	F3(253) = .6	F3(508) = −.6
F3(4) = .8	F3(254) = .4	F3(509) = −.4
F 3(5) = 1.0	F3(255) = .2	F3(510) = −.2
F3(6) = 1.0	F3(256) = 0	F3(511) = 0
. . .	F3(257) = −.2	
	F3(258) = −.4	
	F3(259) = −.6	
	F3(260) = −.8	
	F3(261) = −1.0	
	F3(262) = −1.0	
	. . .	

Fig. 29. Function stored as 512 samples.

indicated as dots on the function. Actually only 511 numbers are independent since F3(0) = F3(511). The 512 numbers representing the function are listed below the function. These numbers are actually stored in 512 locations in the computer memory. The programs that calculate and store the numbers are called GEN routines and will be discussed later.

One may ask, why go to all the trouble of having a GEN program compute and store numbers and then have the ØSC program modify and repeat these numbers? Why not, instead, have the GEN programs repeatedly calculate exactly the desired numbers? The reason, the importance of which cannot be overemphasized, is efficiency. ØSC is a very fast number repeater. The GEN programs must be flexible and, hence, they are in comparison very slow.

By denoting a function F3, we imply that several stored functions are possible. In the training orchestra 10 functions, designated F1 through F10, are available.

The simplest ØSC program would simply repeat the 511 numbers in F3, one after the other: F3(0), F3(1),..., F3(511), F3(1), ... This would produce an oscillation whose peak amplitude would be 1 and whose frequency would be $20,000/511 = 39.14$ Hz. That frequency is too low for most purposes. By repeating every other sample, F3(1), F3(3),..., F3(511), F3(2),..., one could produce a higher frequency, 78.28 Hz. In general, by repeating every nth sample of F3, one obtains a frequency of

$$\frac{20,000}{511} \cdot n \text{ Hz}$$

F3 is stored as samples, as is the output of ØSC: the process carried out by ØSC can be thought of as resampling F3 to obtain a desired frequency. A simple resampling that puts out every nth sample of F3 can produce only frequencies that are multiples of 39.14 Hz. Clearly these offer too limited a choice of frequencies.

The actual algorithm used in ØSC, which overcomes these limitations, is

$$S_{i+1} = S_i + I2_i$$
$$Ø_i = I1_i \cdot F_n([S_i]_{\text{Mod } 511})$$

where

    i is the index of acoustic output samples;

    S_i is a running sum which increases by $I2_i$ for each successive value of i; S_i is usually set to zero at the beginning of each note;

    $[S_i]_{\text{Mod } 511}$ is $[S_i - n \cdot 511]$ where n is selected so that $[S_i]_{\text{Mod } 511}$ always falls between 0 and 511;

    $I1_i$ is the amplitude input that multiplies the amplitude of F_n;

    $I2_i$ is the frequency controlling input; and

    $Ø_i$ is the output.

The operation of ØSC can be understood geometrically by referring to Fig. 30. S_i is a ramp function whose slope is I2 units per sample of acoustic output. $[S_i]_{\text{Mod } 511}$ is the sawtooth function which is reset to zero each time S_i equals a multiple of 511. With a slope of I2, exactly $511/I2$ samples are required for S_i to reach 511; hence the period of $[S_i]_{\text{Mod } 511}$ is exactly $511/I2$ samples. At a sampling rate of 20,000 Hz, the frequency of $[S_i]_{\text{Mod } 511}$ is

$$\text{Freq} = \frac{20,000 \cdot I2}{511}$$

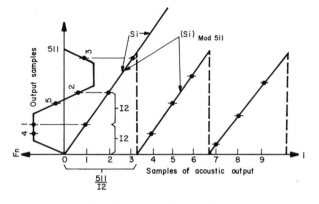

Fig. 30. Operation of ØSC.

This is the fundamental relation between the frequency of ØSC and I2. It can be written

Freq = 39.4·I2

or in case we want to solve for I2 for a given frequency

I2 = .02555·freq

More generally,

$$I2 = \frac{N_F}{R} \cdot freq$$

where N_F is the length of a stored function (N_F = number of samples − 1) and R is the acoustic sampling rate.

[$S_i]_{Mod\,511}$ has the desired frequency but the wrong waveform—a simple triangle. [$S_i]_{Mod}$ is used to scan F_n as specified by the second ØSC equation. The scanning process is equivalent to projecting samples of [$S_i]_{Mod\,511}$ to the left in Fig. 30 and sampling F_n as indicated. This process, along with a multiplication by I1, gives an output of the desired frequency, amplitude, and waveform.

Although [$S_i]_{Mod\,511}$ lies between 0 and 511, it will not, in general, take integer values. Since $F_n(k)$ is sampled and stored only for integer values of k, some accommodation must be made. The simplest ØSC algorithm truncates [$S_i]_{Mod\,511}$ to the next smaller integer value. More complex ØSC routines interpolate $F_n(k)$ between successive k's.

In the score ØSC would be called by a statement such as

ØSC P5 P6 B2 F2 P30 ;

where P5 is the amplitude input, P6 the frequency input, B2 the I-Ø block for output, F2 the stored function, and P30 is a vacant-note parameter location for storing the sum S_i. One of the note record parameters must be reserved for S_i. Since the initial value of S_i is zero, the parameter need not be written; unwritten parameters are always set to zero at the beginning of each note.

Examples of Simple Instruments

Having now discussed the four simplest and most important generators, let us look at some examples of instruments constructed of these generators. For each instrument we will show the score cards which define the instrument and play a note or two. The instruments will require two or more stored functions. Although the GEN score cards that generate these functions are shown here we will postpone until later a detailed discussion of the GEN routines.

We will also postpone discussion of the conversion function which greatly simplifies writing scores of the notes. Consequently, our scores will be somewhat labored and should not be considered typical.

Instrument with Attack and Decay

The simplest instrument shown in Fig. 27 produces sounds by turning an ØSC on and off suddenly. The sudden transients might be heard as unwanted clicks. An instrument is shown in Fig. 31a with an envelope that gradually increases the sound amplitude at the beginning of the note and decreases the amplitude at the end.

The upper ØSC generates the desired envelope which forms the amplitude input for the lower ØSC. F1, the waveform function for the upper ØSC, is the desired envelope as sketched in Fig. 31b. The ØSC is used in a degenerate mode in that its frequency will be set at the value that permits it to go through exactly one cycle of oscillation during the note being played. Usually this is a very low frequency; however, unlike real oscillators, computer-simulated oscillators can produce low frequencies with ease and precision. The frequency-control equation for ØSC is

$$P6 = \frac{511}{20,000} \cdot \text{freq}$$

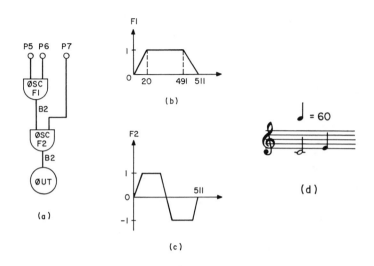

(a)

(b)

(c)

(d)

```
1   INS 0 1 ;
2   ØSC P5 P6 B2 F1 P30 ;
3   ØSC B2 P7 B2 F2 P29 ;
4   ØUT B2 B1 ;
5   END ;
6   GEN 0 1 1 0 0 .99 20 .99 491 0 511 ;
7   GEN 0 1 2 0 0 .99 50 .99 205 −.99 306 −.99 461 0 511 ;
8   NØT 0 1 2 1000 .0128 6.70 ;
9   NØT 2 1 1 1000 .0256 8.44 ;
10  TER 3 ;
```

(e)

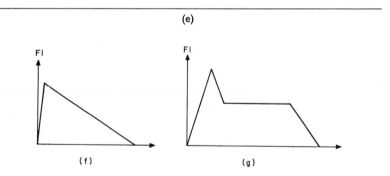

(f)

(g)

Fig. 31. Instrument with attack and decay: (a) block diagram; (b) envelope function; (c) waveform function; (d) conventional score; (e) computer score; (f) pianolike envelope; (g) brasslike envelope.

If we wish exactly one cycle of oscillation per note,

$$\text{Freq} = \frac{1}{\text{note duration}}$$

or

$$P6 = \frac{511}{20,000 \times \text{note duration}}$$

$$= \frac{.02555}{\text{note duration}}$$

Thus, for the first note, whose duration is 2 sec, P6 equals .0128 (line 8 of score) and for the second note, whose duration is 1 sec, P6 equals .0256.

The envelope does much more than eliminate clicks. It is as important in the determination of timbre as the waveform. The attack time is especially important; percussive instruments have very short times (1 or 2 msec), stringed instruments having long times (50–200 msec). In addition, envelopes can have other shapes: the triangular shape shown as an alternate envelope on Fig. 31f is typical of a piano, and the envelope with initial overshoot in Fig. 31g is typical of a brass instrument.

The score, Fig. 31e, is similar to the score in Fig. 27. A few points should be mentioned. The instrument is named "1" and is referred to as "1" in P3 of the NØT cards. I-Ø block B2 is used for both the input and output of the lower ØSC. This is permissible since all the unit generators read their inputs before storing their outputs. However, as will be pointed out later, an I-Ø block must not be used for two different purposes at the same time. The upper ØSC uses P30 to store its S_i; the lower ØSC uses P29. In general, since the S_i's of different ØSC's are different, they must be kept in different locations.

Record 6 causes the generation of the envelope function by evoking GEN1; its operation is the same as in Fig. 27. The envelopes produced by an ØSC have the unfortunate characteristic that the whole envelope stretches and shrinks with the duration of the note. Thus the attack time and the decay time are proportional to duration; the second note in the score will have half the attack time of the first note. Usually this variation is undesirable since it changes the timbre of the note. Special attack and decay generators, which avoid this problem, will be taken up later.

Adding Vibrato

Vibrato, which we will define as a variation in pitch, adds much interest to tone color. In Fig. 32a ØSC #2 and AD2 have been appended to the simple attack and decay instrument to provide vibrato. They

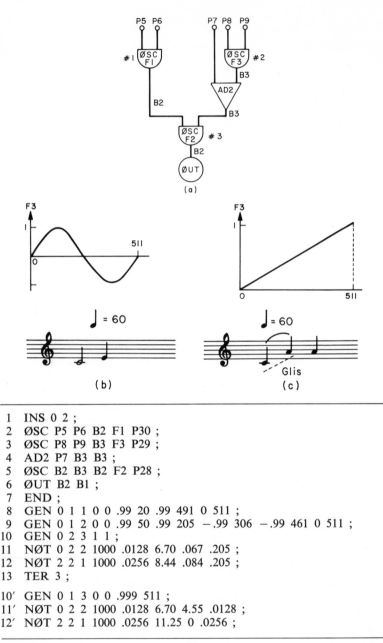

Figure content (a), (b), (c):

```
      P5  P6              P7  P8  P9
       o   o               o   o   o
         ┌─────┐             ┌─────┐
  #1     │ ØSC │        ┌────│ ØSC │ #2
         │  FI │        │    │  F3 │
         └─────┘        │    └─────┘
                        │      │ B3
                        │    ┌────┐
                        │    │AD2 │
                        │    └────┘
              B2        │      │ B3
               │        └──────┤
               │               │
               └───────────────┤ B3
                      ┌─────┐
                      │ ØSC │ #3
                      │  F2 │
                      └─────┘
                        │ B2
                      ┌────┐
                      │ØUT │
                      └────┘
                       (a)
```

(b) F3 sine wave, 0 to 511, ♩ = 60, score

(c) F3 linear ramp, 0 to 511, ♩ = 60, score, Glis

```
 1   INS 0 2 ;
 2   ØSC P5 P6 B2 F1 P30 ;
 3   ØSC P8 P9 B3 F3 P29 ;
 4   AD2 P7 B3 B3 ;
 5   ØSC B2 B3 B2 F2 P28 ;
 6   ØUT B2 B1 ;
 7   END ;
 8   GEN 0 1 1 0 0 .99 20 .99 491 0 511 ;
 9   GEN 0 1 2 0 0 .99 50 .99 205 −.99 306 −.99 461 0 511 ;
10   GEN 0 2 3 1 1 ;
11   NØT 0 2 2 1000 .0128 6.70 .067 .205 ;
12   NØT 2 2 1 1000 .0256 8.44 .084 .205 ;
13   TER 3 ;

10′  GEN 0 1 3 0 0 .999 511 ;
11′  NØT 0 2 2 1000 .0128 6.70 4.55 .0128 ;
12′  NØT 2 2 1 1000 .0256 11.25 0 .0256 ;
```

(d)

Fig. 32. Instruments with vibrato or glissando: (a) block diagram; (b) F3 and score for vibrato; (c) F3 and score for glissando; (d) computer score.

provide a time-varying frequency control to ØSC #3, thus producing a frequency variation in its output. This illustrates that the frequency control of an ØSC does not have to remain constant over a note, but can change in any desired way. P7 controls the average pitch. P8 determines the maximum variation in pitch. P9 determines the rate of variations, which for typical instruments might be 4 to 8 changes per second. The waveshape F3 of ØSC #2 determines the way in which frequency changes with time. The exact shape is usually not critical and a sine wave, as shown, is usually satisfactory.

In the first score card, Fig. 32d, the instrument is named "2" and referred to as such in the P3 fields of the NØT records. An additional I-Ø block B3 is required by the instrument. Block B2 must hold the output of ØSC #1 until ØSC #3 has used it as amplitude input. Consequently, ØSC #2 and AD2 has to use B3 to hold the frequency input for ØSC #3. However, after ØSC #3 has completed its computation, both B2 and B3 are available for other uses; in this case B2 was used to hold the output of ØSC #3.

The order of computation is the order in which generators are written in the score. It is essential to maintain the right order. In the example, ØSC #1 must be written ahead of ØSC #3 since it provides an input to ØSC #3. ØSC #2 must be written ahead of AD2, and AD2 must be ahead of ØSC #3 for the same reason. ØSC #1 could be in any order with respect to ØSC #2 and AD2.

The two GEN1 functions (records 8 and 9) are the same as before. Record 10 calls upon GEN2 to provide a sine wave for F3. P2 = 0 says to compute F3 at t = 0 with respect to the acoustic output. P3 = 2 says to call upon GEN2; P4 = 3 says to compute F3; P5 = 1 says to compute the fundamental with amplitude of 1; P6 = 1 says that there is only one harmonic (i.e., the fundamental).

In note records 11 and 12, P7, P8, and P9 concern pitch and hence are of special interest. The rest of the parameters are the same as in Fig. 31. P7 determines average pitch. Thus for the first note C_{262}

$$P7 = 262 \times .02555 = 6.70$$

P8 is set equal to 1% of P7 so that the maximum frequency deviation will be 1% of the center frequency. Thus the frequency will change from 259.4 Hz to 264.6 Hz. A 1% vibrato is quite large; $\frac{3}{4}$% is more typical of actual players. However, there is much individual variation in vibrato. P9 determines the number of complete cycles of change per second, which we have set at 8. Thus

$$P9 = 8 \times .02555 = .205$$

With a change in F3, and the meaning of P7, P8, and P9, the same instrument can also be used for glissando. An F3 consisting of a straight "interpolating" function appropriate for glissando is shown in Fig. 32c. P9 now becomes

$$P9 = \frac{.0255}{\text{duration of note}}$$

and causes ØSC #2 to produce one cycle per note (the same as ØSC #1). P7 is set at

$$P7 = .0255 \times \text{initial note frequency}$$

and P8 at

$$P8 = .0255 \times (\text{final note frequency} - \text{initial note frequency})$$

The action of AD2 and ØSC #2 with F3 is such that at the beginning of the note B3 will contain .0255 × initial note frequency, and at the end of the note it will contain .0255 × final note frequency.

Substitution of cards 10', 11', and 12' into the score in place of cards 10, 11, and 12 will produce the glissando sample shown. Note that for the second note (A_{440}), which has a constant frequency, P8 is equal to 0 since the initial and final frequencies are the same. P6 and P9 have the same values, and hence P9 could be eliminated if the instrument were redefined.

The glissando obtained in this way has a linear change of frequency in hertz. This means that the musical intervals will change faster at the beginning of the slide than at the end. Although a linear change of musical intervals might be preferable, this glissando has been much used and seems perfectly satisfactory. During most slides, listeners are insensitive to the precise time course of the pitch.

Instrument with Swell and Diminuendo

In the glissando instrument, ØSC #2 and AD2 form a linear interpolating unit which generates a frequency control that goes from initial to final frequency. If we apply the interpolating unit to the amplitude control on an ØSC, we can obtain a continuously changing amplitude for crescendos and decrescendos. An instrument with this feature is shown in Fig. 33.

In order to simplify the score, we have complicated the interpolater with an extra oscillator ØSC #2. The glissando instrument required writing the initial frequency in P7 and the (final-initial) frequency in P8. The swelling instrument is arranged so the initial amplitude is

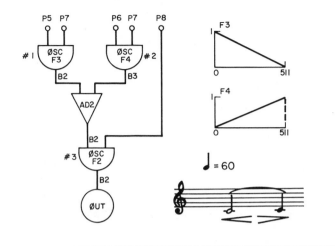

```
 1   INS 0 3 ;
 2   ØSC P5 P7 B2 F3 P30 ;
 3   ØSC P6 P7 B3 F4 P29 ;
 4   AD2 B2 B3 B2 ;
 5   ØSC B2 P8 B2 F2 V1 ;
 6   ØUT B2 B1 ;
 7   END ;
 8   GEN 0 1 3 .999 0 0 511 ;
 9   GEN 0 1 4 0 0 .999 511 ;
10   GEN 0 1 2 0 0 .99 50 .99 205  −.99 306  −.99 461 0 511 ;
11   NØT 0 3 2 0 2000 .0128 6.70 ;
12   NØT 2 3 1 2000 0 .0256 6.70 ;
13   TER 3 ;
```

Fig. 33. Instrument with swell and diminuendo.

written in P5 and the final amplitude in P6. ØSC #1 and ØSC #2 both generate one cycle per note of waveforms F3 and F4, respectively. F3 goes linearly from 1 to 0 over the course of a note and is multiplied by the initial amplitude in ØSC #1. Similarly, F4 goes from 0 to 1 and is multiplied by the final amplitude. Thus the output of AD2 will proceed linearly from the initial amplitude to the final amplitude.

Records 11 and 12 in the score play what amounts to a single note made up of two notes tied together. The first note swells from 0 to maximum amplitude, the second decays back to zero. Amplitude controls in P5 and P6 are obvious. P7 is set to produce one cycle per note in both ØSC #1 and ØSC #2.

One peculiarity is introduced by the structure and use of the instrument. We want the two notes to blend into each other with no break between notes. To achieve this, we have omitted the usual attack and decay ØSC. However, the waveform ØSC #3 must also produce a continuous output over the juncture. If we were to store the sum for the ØSC in an unused note parameter (P30, for example), it would be reset to zero at the beginning of each note, a sudden change of phase between notes would result, and a click might be introduced. To avoid this transient, the sum is stored in variable V1. The training orchestra provides space for 200 variables, denoted V1 through V200. These variables may be changed by either the instruments or the score, but they are not reset at the beginning of a note. Consequently, storing the sum of ØSC #3 in V1 assures that it will never be reset and that the oscillator will proceed continuously between all notes. However, this instrument will be limited to playing only one voice.

There are many other uses for variables, as we will see in the next example.

Instrument that Varies Waveform with Amplitude

We conclude these examples of simple instruments with a not-so-simple one. It has been shown that one of the factors that contribute interest to the timbre of real instruments is a change in spectrum with the intensity of the sound. Usually the loud sounds have more high-frequency components than the soft sounds. Figure 34 shows an instrument that is able to change spectrum with amplitude.

The instrument is an elaboration of the swell and diminuendo instrument shown in Fig. 33, and it uses the same parameters on the note records. ØSC #1, ØSC #2, and AD2 #1 form a linear interpolation unit with P5 as the initial amplitude and P6 the final amplitude. These inputs range from 0 to 1 with 1 as the maximum output. We will call the instantaneous amplitude Amp_1. Amp_1 is stored in block B2. MLT #1 and AD2 compute B3 according to the relation

$$B3 = 1 - Amp_1 = Amp_2$$

Oscillator ØSC #4 is controlled by Amp_1, and ØSC #5 by Amp_2. Thus when Amp_1 is 0, Amp_2 is equal to 1, and all the output comes from ØSC #5; when Amp_1 is 1, Amp_2 is equal to 0, and all output comes from ØSC #4. At intermediate values of Amp_1, intermediate portions of output come from ØSC #5 and ØSC #4. In this way the waveform of F2 in ØSC #5 controls the spectrum at low amplitudes, and the waveform of F1 in ØSC #6 controls at high amplitudes.

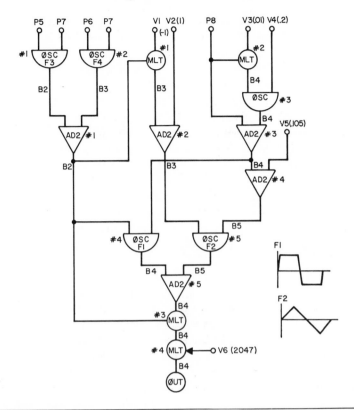

```
 1   INS 0 4 ;
 2   ØSC P5 P7 B2 F3 P30 ;
 3   ØSC P6 P7 B3 F4 P29 ;
 4   AD2 B2 B3 B2 ;
 5   MLT B2 V1 B3 ;
 6   AD2 B3 V2 B3 ;
 7   MLT P8 V3 B4 ;
 8   ØSC B4 V4 B4 F5 P28 ;
 9   AD2 P8 B4 B4 ;
10   AD2 B4 V5 B5 ;
11   ØSC B3 B5 B5 F2 V7 ;
12   ØSC B2 B4 B4 F1 V8 ;
13   MLT B2 B4 B4 ;
14   MLT B4 V6 B4 ;
15   ØUT B4 B1 ;
16   END ;
```

Fig. 34. Instrument that varies waveform with amplitude.

The amplitude of the sum of ØSC #4 and ØSC #5 is relatively independent of Amp$_1$. The normal dependence is restored by MLT #3. The output of MLT #3 ranges from -1 to $+1$; MLT #4 increases this range to -2047 to $+2047$, the normal amplitude range.

Frequency control of ØSC #4 and ØSC #5 is a vibrato circuit plus AD2 #4, which makes ØSC #5 4 Hz higher in frequency than ØSC #4. A slight divergence adds richness to the tone. The amplitude of the vibrato is automatically set at 1% of the center frequency of the tone by MLT #2. This is an expensive way of controlling amplitude, and better ways will be discussed when CØNVT functions are considered. The frequency of vibrato is set at about 6 Hz by V4.

The instrument requires six constants as inputs. These are stored in V1 through V6: V1 $= -1$, V2 $= 1$, V3 $= .01$, V4 $= .2$, V5 $= .105$, and V6 $= 2047$. The record that stores these constants is

SV3 0 1 -1 1 .01 .2 .105 2047;

P1 and P2 say to set variables in Pass III at time 0. P3 says to start with variable 1 and continue with 2, 3, etc., to the end of the data. P4–P9 give the six numbers to be set in V1–V6. New variables can be set at any time, as previously set variables can be changed, with other SV3 cards. Times of settings and changes are all controlled by P2.

We will not write a score for this instrument since, except for setting variables, little new is involved. A reasonable choice for F1 and F2 is sketched in Fig. 34. The harmonics of F1 decrease at about 6 dB per octave; those of F2 at 12 dB per octave. Thus the instrument is likely to have higher-frequency energy at high output amplitudes. Other more interesting examples of F1 and F2 could be devised.

CØNVT Function to Process Note Parameters

Scores for the instruments thus far discussed contain many affronts to a lazy composer, and all composers should be as lazy as possible when writing scores. For example, computing the frequency control of an oscillator as

I2 $= .02555 \times$ frequency in hertz

is a tedious process. Instead, one would like to write the notes of a scale directly, such as the numbers 0–11 for a 12-tone scale.

A FØRTRAN routine named CØNVT is called at the end of Pass II; it can apply the full power of FØRTRAN to convert the note parameters as written by the composer into a new set of parameters, which are the inputs to the instruments. As will be clear from the examples below, the nature of CØNVT depends on the instruments used with it. Consequently, no universal CØNVT program is or can be supplied with Music V; instead the composer must write his own for each orchestra he defines. Let us explore the possibilities with the simple attack and decay instrument designed in Fig. 31.

We shall assume that the composer would like to write frequency directly in hertz and would like to write amplitude on a decibel scale rather than on a linear scale. Furthermore, the note duration is already written in P4; it is an indignity to have to write P6 ($= .02555/$duration). Hence we will assume that the composer will write

P5 = amplitude of note in decibels with 66 dB corresponding to a maximum amplitude of 2000

P6 = frequency of note in hertz

With these inputs CØNVT must compute[2]

P5 = 10.0**(P5/20.0)

P7 = 511.0 * P6/(sampling rate)

and

P6 = 511.0/(P4 * sampling rate)

A program to achieve these conversions is given below along with annotated comments.

Text	Notes
SUBRØUTINE CØNVT	
CØMMØN IP, P, G	1
DIMENSIØN IP(10), P(100), G(1000)	
IF (P(1) − 1.0) 102, 100, 102	2
100 IF (P(3) − 1.0) 102, 101, 102	3
101 P(5) = 10.0 ** (P(5)/20.0)	4
P(7) = 511.0 * P(6)/G(4)	
P(6) = 511.0/(P(4) * G(4))	
IP(1) = 7	5
102 RETURN	
END	

Notes
1. The data-record parameters P1–P100 have been placed by Pass II in P(1)–P(100). The IP array contains some pertinent fixed-point

[2] Equations relating to programs will usually be written in a FØRTRAN-like notation.

constants; in particular, IP(1) = number of parameters in the data record. G is a general memory array for Pass II.

2. This statement checks to see whether the data record pertains to a note (rather than a GEN or something else). The numerical equivalent of NØT is 1. Chapter 3, Section 3 lists the numerical equivalent of all the operation codes.

3. This statement checks to see whether instrument #1 is referred to by the NØT record. Other instruments would usually require other CØNVT functions.

4. These statements perform the desired conversions. The sampling rate is always kept in variable G(4). Thus in calculating P(6) and P(7) we have divided by G(4) rather than by the number 20,000. This is desirable because sampling rate is often changed and, if CØNVT always refers to G(4) to obtain the current rate, it will not have to be reassembled with each change of rate. Instead only G(4) need be modified, and this is a simple change which we will discuss shortly.

5. CØNVT has added one parameter P(7); thus the word count IP(1) must be changed to 7. The possibility of *generating additional parameters with CØNVT* is most important and attractive since the composer does not have to write these parameters. In addition, Pass I and Pass II do not have to process and sort these additions, which increases efficiency.

With this CØNVT function the score lines to play the two notes on Fig. 31d (equivalent to lines 8 and 9 on Fig. 31c) are

    NØT 0 1 2 60 262 ;
    NØT 2 1 1 60 330 ;

Now let us construct a somewhat more complicated CØNVT function for instrument 2 in Fig. 32. We will again use P5 as amplitude in decibels. Frequency will be specified in terms of an octave, and a 12-tone note within the octave by P6 and P7, P6 giving the octave and P7 the step within the octave. Thus, for example

Note	P6	P7
C_{131}	-1	0
C#	-1	1
D	-1	2
...		

B	−1	11
C_{262}	0	0
C#	0	1
...		
C_{524}	1	0

The vibrato controls will be eliminated from the NØT record. Instead, we will assign two Pass II variables, G(50) to control the percent frequency variation and G(51) the rate of vibrato.

The equations which must be programmed into CØNVT are

Frequency = 262.0 ∗ (2 ∗∗ (P6 + P7/12.0))

P5 = 10.0 ∗∗ (P5/20.0)

P6 = 511.0/(P4 ∗ sampling rate)

P7 = 511.0 ∗ frequency/sampling rate

P8 = 511.0 ∗ frequency ∗ G(50)/(sampling rate ∗ 100)

P9 = 511.0 ∗ G(51)/sampling rate

Most of the equations are self-explanatory. The note frequency is computed in hertz from the logarithmic scales embodied in P6 and P7 by the first relation. The factor 100 is put in the denominator of P8 because G(50) is a percentage.

Vibrato control is a good example of the use of Pass II memory in a composition. Except for the first few variables, numbers in the G array may be used for any purpose desired by the composer. Numbers are placed in the array by an SV2 record, which is analogous to the SV3 record that was previously used to set a Pass III variable. Thus

SV2 0 50 .5 6 ;

would set G(50) = .5 and G(51) = 6 at t = 0.

The program to carry out the computations follows.

	Text	Notes

SUBRØUTINE CØNVT	
CØMMØN IP, P, G	
DIMENSIØN IP(10), P(100), G(1000)	
IF (P(1) − 1.0) 102, 100, 102	
100 IF (P(3) − 2.0) 102, 101, 102	
101 P(5) = 10.0 ∗∗ (P(5)/20.0)	
P(7) = 511.0 ∗ 262.0 ∗ (2.0 ∗∗ (P(6) + P(7)/12.0))/G(4)	1
P(6) = 511.0/(P(4) ∗ G(4))	
P(8) = P(7) ∗ G(50)/100.0	2
P(9) = G(51) ∗ 511.0/G(4)	3
IP(2) = 9	
102 RETURN	
END	

Notes
1. This statement calculates frequency, multiples it by the appropriate constant of proportionality, and stores it in P(7).
2. This statement computes the maximum vibrato deviation. The properly scaled frequency is already available in P(7) and hence must only be multiplied by G(50)/100.0.
3. This statement sets the rate of vibrato. The constant of proportionality, 511.0/G(4), is the same as any other ØSC frequency control. G(51) will be the vibrato frequency in hertz.

A score for this instrument to replace lines 11 and 12 on Fig. 32 is

```
SV2  0 50 1  6 ;
NØT 0  2 2 60 0 0 ;
NØT 2  2 1 60 0 4 ;
```

Once G(50) and G(51) are set, any number of notes may be written with the same vibrato. On the other hand, the vibrato constants may be changed at any time by a subsequent SV2 record. For example, the deviation could be reduced and the rate increased at t = 15 sec by the record

```
SV2 15 50 .5 8 ;
```

One may ask, why use Pass II variables in CØNVT rather than Pass III variables or Pass I variables which also exist? The answer is, CØNVT is a Pass II subroutine and can only make use of information available in Pass II.

A final example of a CØNVT subroutine will provide a convenient score language for the glissando instrument in Fig. 32. As shown, the initial frequency of a note must be written in P7 and the (final − initial) frequency in P8. We shall eliminate the arithmetic to calculate (final − initial). Instead the score card will have

P5 = amplitude in decibels

and

P6 = final frequency in hertz

The initial frequency of each note will be defined as the final frequency of the preceding note. The initial frequency of the first note will be read into the program with an SV2 card into G(50).

In order to use this simple form the program must remember the final frequency of each note. G(50) will also be used for this purpose.

The program to achieve these objectives follows.

Text	Notes

```
     SUBRØUTINE CØNVT
     CØMMØN IP, P, G
     DIMENSION IP (10), P(100), G(1000)
     IF (P(1) − 1.0) 102, 100, 102
100  IF (P(3) − 2.0) 102, 101, 102
101  P(5) = 10.0 ** (P(5)/20.0)
     P(7) = G(50) * 511.0/G(4)                    1
     P(8) = (P(6) − G(50)) * 511.0/G(4)           2
     G(50) = P(6)                                 3
     P(6) = 511.0/(P(4) * G(4))                   4
     P(9) = P(6)
     IP(2) = 9
102  RETURN
     END
```

Notes

1. This statement sets the initial frequency, which was stored in G(50).
2. This statement computes the (final − initial) frequency.
3. This statement stores the final frequency in G(50) to become the initial frequency of the next note.
4. This and the following statement set the frequency inputs of ØSC #1 and #2 to 1 cycle per note.

Figure 35 shows a brief score for the instrument. Only the NØT cards and the SV2 cards are shown. Record 1 sets the initial frequency

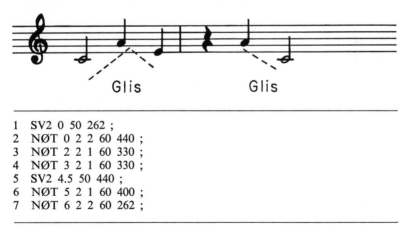

```
1   SV2 0 50 262 ;
2   NØT 0 2 2 60 440 ;
3   NØT 2 2 1 60 330 ;
4   NØT 3 2 1 60 330 ;
5   SV2 4.5 50 440 ;
6   NØT 5 2 1 60 400 ;
7   NØT 6 2 2 60 262 ;
```

Fig. 35. Score for glissando instrument using a CØNVT subroutine.

to 262 Hz. Records 2, 3, and 4 generate an initial glissando. An arbitrary choice is made. The frequency slide is completed at t = 3, and the third note is held at E 330. Record 5 resets the initial frequency to 440 for the beginning of the second glissando. The change is done at t = 4.5 in the middle of a rest and hence is inaudible. A different arbitrary choice for glissando is made for the last two notes. During the first note (5 < t < 6), the frequency changes from 440 to 400. During the second note (6 < t < 8) the frequency shift continues from 400 to 262.

The flexibility of one method for obtaining frequency slides has been demonstrated. The use of Pass II variables as a memory for the CØNVT subroutine is important. Powerful logic may be programmed in this way.

Additional Unit Generators—RAN, ENV, FLT

Next to be discussed are the generator of random signals RAN, the band-pass filter FLT, and the envelope generator ENV. Although a few other generators exist and one can easily design his own generators, the three described here plus the stereo output box are sufficient for most purposes.

Random Signal Generator—RAN

RAN is a source of random signals with controlled amplitude and spectrum. The spectrum is low pass and contains energy from zero frequency to a cutoff frequency determined by one of the inputs (I2). (As will be shown later, RAN may be combined with an oscillator to obtain a band-pass signal.)

The diagram of RAN is shown in Fig. 36a. I1 controls the amplitude of $\emptyset$; I2 controls its bandwidth. The equation of operation is

$$\emptyset_i = I1_i \cdot R_i(I2_i)$$

where $R_i(I2_i)$ is a low-pass random function whose amplitude varies from -1 to $+1$ and whose cutoff frequency is approximately $(R \cdot I2)/1024$ where R is the sampling rate. The amplitude of $\emptyset_i$ varies from $-I1_i$ to $I1_i$. The approximate spectrum of $\emptyset$ is shown in Fig. 36b. The cutoff frequency is not abrupt, and there are lobes of energy above $(R \cdot I2)/1024$ Hz. Neither does the main passband have a flat top. Even with these deficiencies, the generator is very useful.

The key to RAN is the generation of the random function R_i. This is obtained by generating a sequence of independent random numbers N_i, which are uniformly distributed over the interval -1 to $+1$. These

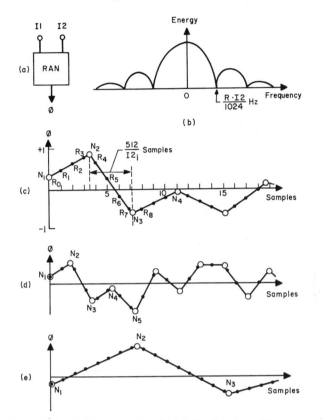

Fig. 36. Random generator—RAN: (a) block diagram; (b) spectrum of Ø; (c) medium-frequency random function; (d) high-frequency random function; (e) low-frequency random function.

numbers are connected by straight lines to form the continuous functions shown in Fig. 36c. R_i consists of samples of the line function, the sampling interval being chosen so that $512/I2_i$ sampling intervals fall between each N_i ($512/I2_i$ does not need to be an integer). The algorithm for sampling the line function is similar to the sum in ØSC.

A medium-frequency function with $I2 \simeq 128$ is shown in Fig. 36c. It wiggles at a moderate rate and at $R = 20,000$ Hz would have a cutoff of about 2500 Hz.

A high-frequency function with $I2 \simeq 256$ and a cutoff of 5000 Hz is shown in Fig. 36d. The N_i independent random numbers occur more frequently here, giving the function a more jagged appearance and a higher-frequency spectrum. The maximum useful value of I2 is 512.

This will produce an independent number for each sample and will achieve a cutoff of R/2, which is the highest frequency representable by R samples per second.

A low-frequency function with $I2_i \cong 64$ and a cutoff of 1250 Hz is shown in Fig. 36e. It is clearly the smoothest of the three functions.

A score record to evoke RAN is

RAN P5 P6 B2 P30 P29 P28 ;

where P5 is the I1 input, P6 the I2 input, B2 the output; P30 is an unused note parameter for the storage of the sum; and P29 and P28 are two other temporary storage locations.

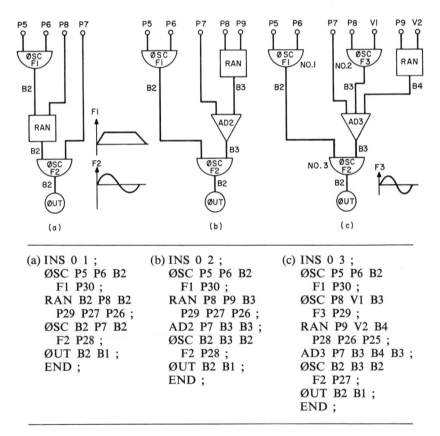

(a) INS 0 1 ;	(b) INS 0 2 ;	(c) INS 0 3 ;
ØSC P5 P6 B2	ØSC P5 P6 B2	ØSC P5 P6 B2
F1 P30 ;	F1 P30 ;	F1 P30 ;
RAN B2 P8 B2	RAN P8 P9 B3	ØSC P8 V1 B3
P29 P27 P26 ;	P29 P27 P26 ;	F3 P29 ;
ØSC B2 P7 B2	AD2 P7 B3 B3 ;	RAN P9 V2 B4
F2 P28 ;	ØSC B2 B3 B2	P28 P26 P25 ;
ØUT B2 B1 ;	F2 P28 ;	AD3 P7 B3 B4 B3 ;
END ;	ØUT B2 B1 ;	ØSC B2 B3 B2
	END ;	F2 P27 ;
		ØUT B2 B1 ;
		END ;

Fig. 37. Examples of instruments with random generator: (a) amplitude-modulated band-pass noise; (b) frequency-modulated band-pass noise; (c) periodic plus random vibrato.

Three useful instruments involving RAN are shown in Fig. 37. Instrument 1 produces a band-pass noise by amplitude modulation of an ØSC with RAN. Both the center frequency and the width of the pass-band are controlled by note parameters, P7 determining the center frequency and P8 the width.

The top ØSC produces the initial attack and decay with function F1. The bottom ØSC has a sinusoidal waveform F2, and without RAN it would produce a single-frequency sinusoid at $R \cdot P7/511$ Hz. By virtue of the multiplication inherent in the amplitude input to ØSC, the sinusoid is multiplied by the output of RAN. Thus the output of RAN is modulated by the sinusoid and according to the convolution theorem (Appendix B) the band-pass spectrum sketched in Fig. 38 is achieved.

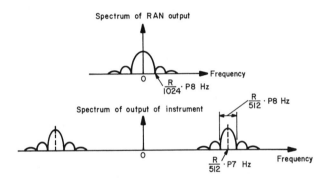

Fig. 38. Spectrum of instrument that generates amplitude-modulated band-pass noise.

The modulation can be looked upon as shifting the (low-pass) spectrum of RAN and centering it about the frequency of ØSC.

If F2 is a complex wave with harmonics, the modulation will generate a replica of the RAN spectrum centered about each harmonic, or a multiple-band noise. Because the auditory effect is usually muddy and unpleasant, most instruments use a sinusoidal F2.

The center frequency of the passband is simply the frequency of ØSC—$R \cdot P7/511$. The bandwidth is two times the cutoff frequency of RAN or $R \cdot P8/512$. The factor 2 comes from the negative frequencies in the RAN spectrum which are shifted into positive frequencies by the modulation. The CØNVT function appropriate to this operation is

$$P7 = \frac{511}{R} \cdot \text{center frequency}$$

and

$$P8 = \frac{512}{R} \cdot \text{bandwidth}$$

It is often desirable to make the bandwidth a fixed percentage of the center frequency. This corresponds to a fixed musical interval about the center frequency. The CØNVT equation is simply

$$P8 = k \cdot P7$$

and P8 must not be written in the score.

Very narrow bands of noise can be generated by small values of P8. In fact, for P8 = 0, a zero bandwidth or pure sinusoid is produced. Narrow-band noises produced by amplitude modulation reveal the way in which they are generated; they sound like a sinusoid with a fluctuating amplitude. This sound is often not what the composer desires or expects from such noises; however, it is an essential characteristic of amplitude modulation and cannot be avoided with this instrument.

INS 2 (Fig. 37b) generates frequency-modulated noise with a band-pass spectrum. The center frequency of the band is again controlled by P7 as $P7 \cdot R/511$. The rest of the characteristics of the spectrum are not as easy to estimate as in the case of the amplitude modulated noise. $P8 \cdot R/511$ is the maximum instantaneous deviation of frequency of ØSC. Frequency-modulation theory says that the width of the noise band will be somewhat greater than $2 \cdot P8 \cdot R/511$. For most purposes $2 \cdot P8 \cdot R/511$ is a useful estimate of bandwidth.

P9 determines the rate at which the frequency of ØSC deviates. Its effect on the spectrum is hard to compute precisely. Experience has indicated that in order to produce "smooth" sounding noise, P9 should be about five times P8. CØNVT is a convenient place to set both P8 and P9.

At very small bandwidths, INS 2 sounds like a sine wave with a small random variation in frequency.

INS 3 (Fig. 37c) shows an excellent vibrato circuit devised by J. C. Tenney. The frequency variation contains a periodic component supplied by ØSC #2 and a random component supplied by RAN. A useful set of parameters is

$$P8 = P9 = .0075 * P7$$

to give $\frac{3}{4}$-percent periodic and $\frac{3}{4}$-percent random variation

$$V1 = 8 * 511/R$$

for an 8-Hz periodic vibration rate and

$$V2 = 16 * 511/R$$

for a 16-Hz random bandwidth. The random bandwidth tends to be substantially greater than the periodic frequency.

Envelope Generator—ENV

The use of ØSC as an envelope generator is satisfactory in some applications, but it makes the attack and decay times proportional to the total note duration. Important aspects of timbre depend on the absolute attack time. With ØSC, these will change from long notes to short notes. The difference may be enough to give the impression of two different kinds of instruments.

A special generator ENV has been programmed to sweep away this limitation. It allows separate control of attack time, steady-state duration, and decay time. In order for ENV to be effective, a special CØNVT function must be written for ENV. The computations in CØNVT are at least as complex as those in ENV.

An instrument using ENV is illustrated in Fig. 39. ENV has four inputs I1–I4 and requires one function. I1 determines the amplitude of the output, and I2, I3, and I4 the attack time, the steady-state time, and the decay time, respectively. The function F1 is divided into four equal sections, the first determining the shape of the attack, the second the shape of the steady state, and the third the shape of the decay. The last section is not used and should be zero to allow for any round-off error involved in scanning the first three parts.

The output $\emptyset_1$ may be written

$$\emptyset_1 = I1_i * \text{function (scanned according to I1, I2, and I3)}$$

The first quarter of the function is scanned at a rate of I2 locations per sample, the second quarter at a rate of I3 locations per sample, and the third quarter at a rate of I4 locations per sample. Consequently, CØNVT should compute

$$I2 = \frac{128}{\text{attack time} * \text{sampling rate}}$$

$$I3 = \frac{128}{\text{steady-state time} * \text{sampling rate}}$$

and

$$I4 = \frac{128}{\text{decay time} * \text{sampling rate}}$$

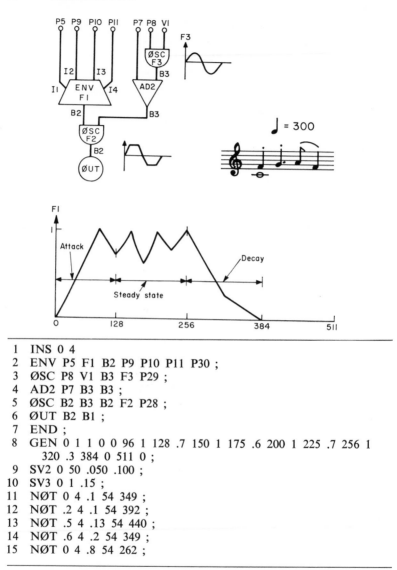

1   INS 0 4
2   ENV P5 F1 B2 P9 P10 P11 P30 ;
3   ØSC P8 V1 B3 F3 P29 ;
4   AD2 P7 B3 B3 ;
5   ØSC B2 B3 B2 F2 P28 ;
6   ØUT B2 B1 ;
7   END ;
8   GEN 0 1 1 0 0 96 1 128 .7 150 1 175 .6 200 1 225 .7 256 1
        320 .3 384 0 511 0 ;
9   SV2 0 50 .050 .100 ;
10 SV3 0 1 .15 ;
11 NØT 0 4 .1 54 349 ;
12 NØT .2 4 .1 54 392 ;
13 NØT .5 4 .13 54 440 ;
14 NØT .6 4 .2 54 349 ;
15 NØT 0 4 .8 54 262 ;

Fig. 39. Envelope generator ENV for attack and decay. Instrument #4.

The attack time AT and decay time DT will in general be constants. CØNVT calculates the steady-state time SS as the duration P(4) minus the attack and decay times

$$SS = P(4) - AT - DT$$

Thus the steady-state time varies with duration. For short notes there may be no steady state, and the attack and decay times may have to be shortened so that their sum does not exceed the duration. All this must be done by CØNVT.

The data record to evoke ENV is

ENV I1, F, Ø, I2, I3, I4, S ;

S is a sum that must be assigned temporary storage in some unused note parameter.

In the example shown in Fig. 39, Pass II variables V50 and V51 contain the attack and decay times, respectively. These are set with the SV2 record. The vibrato rate is kept in Pass III V1 and is set with SV3 record. The attack and decay function F1 is computed with GEN1. The attack portion has a slight overshoot for added sharpness. The steady-state portion has two cycles of quaver. The decay portion has two line segments to approximate an exponential.

The NØT records contain amplitude in decibels in P5 and the frequency in hertz in P6.

The instrument requires inputs P5 and P7 through P11, as shown on the diagram. The CØNVT program to compute these inputs from the NØT record is listed and annotated below.

Text	Notes
SUBRØUTINE CØNVT	
CØMMØN IP, P, G	
DIMENSIØN IP(10), P(100), G(1000)	
IF (P(1) − 1.0) 105, 100, 105	
100 IF (P(3) − 4.0) 105, 101, 105	
101 COR = 1.0	1
SS = P(2) − G(50) − G(51)	
IF (SS) 102, 103, 103	2
102 CØR = P(4)/(G(50) + G(51))	3
P(10) = 128.	
GØ TØ 104	
103 P(10) = 128./(G(4) * SS)	4
104 P(9) = 128./(G(4) * G(50) * COR)	5
P(11) = 128./(G(4) * G(51) * COR)	
P(5) = 10.0 ** (P(5)/20.0)	6
P(7) = 511.0 * P(6)/G(4)	
P(8) = .0075 * P(7)	
IP(1) = 11	
105 RETURN	
END	

Notes

1. CØR will correct attack and decay times for short notes where the steady state does not exist.
2. Checks to see if steady state time SS is positive.
3. Steady state is negative. CØR is set to reduce attack and decay times proportionally so that

    AT + DT = duration

    P(10) is set at 128 so that steady-state time will equal one sample, which is the minimum possible steady state.
4. Computation of P(10) for positive steady-state times.
5. Computation of P(9) and P(11) for either positive or zero steady-state times. CØR will be less than 1 for zero steady-state times.
6. The usual computation of amplitude and frequency control. Vibrato amplitude is set at $\frac{3}{4}$ percent of center frequency.

The NØT records (11–15) play the five notes sketched on the staff. Two additional capabilities of the program are inherent in these records. Instrument #4 is used to play up to three voices simultaneously. The second voice is a sustained C_{262}. The third voice occurs because the slurred notes overlap slightly, with the note from record 6 extending into the beginning of the note from record 7. Pass III can play multiple simultaneous voices on any instrument. As many as 30 voices can be played in the training orchestra.

The score records are not written in ascending sequence of action times, in that the C_{262} is written last and starts at t = 0. The order of these records is immaterial, since they will be sorted into the proper ascending sequence of action times in Pass II.

Filter—FLT

One of the more difficult sound-processing operations is filtering. A unit generator that operates as a band-pass filter is shown in Fig. 40. The filter may be used to introduce formants or energy peaks at specified frequencies into sound waves. Such formants are characteristic of many instruments.

The filter is calculated by means of a difference equation. In terms of the diagram shown in Fig. 40, the equation is

$$\emptyset_i = I1_i + I2_i \cdot \emptyset_{i-1} - I3_i \cdot \emptyset_{i-2}$$

I1 is the input to the filter, $\emptyset$ the output, and I2 and I3 determine the frequency and bandwidth of the passband.

More specifically, the difference equation approximates a 2-pole filter with a pole pair at $-D \pm j\,F$ Hz on the complex frequency plane

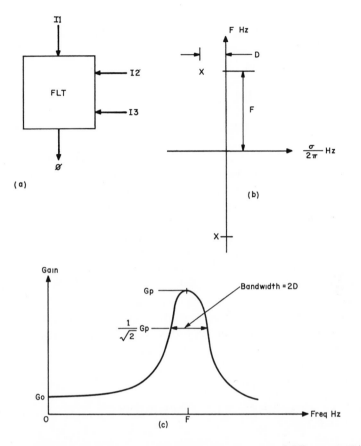

Fig. 40. Band-pass filter—FLT. (a) Diagram: $I2 = 2e^{-2\pi D/R} \cos 2\pi F/R$; $I3 = e^{-4\pi D/R}$; (b) poles in complex plane; (c) curve of gain vs. frequency.

as shown in Fig. 40. The approximate gain of the filter is also shown as a function of frequency in Fig. 40, where the peak occurs at F Hz and the bandwidth at the half-power points is 2D Hz. The approximation holds for $F \gg D$. I2 and I3 are determined as functions of F and D by the relations

$$I2 = 2\,e^{-2\pi D/R} \cos 2\pi F/R$$

and

$$I3 = e^{-4\pi D/R}$$

where R is the sampling rate. CØNVT may be conveniently used to compute I2 and I3 from F and D.

The main problem in using the filter is obtaining a reasonable amplitude of output. The dc gain G_0 is given by the equation

$$G_0 = \frac{1}{1 - I2 + I3}$$

and the peak gain is approximately

$$G_p = G_0 \cdot \frac{F}{2D} \qquad \text{for } F \gg D$$

Both gains may be either less than or much greater than unity, depending on F and D. Narrow bandwidths produce high peak gains.

The amplitude of the output depends both on the amplitude of the input and on its frequency composition. A sinusoid near frequency F will be multiplied by G_p. A low-frequency sinusoid will be multiplied by G_0. A complex signal must be decomposed into individual harmonics, the gain for each harmonic computed separately, and the resulting amplified harmonics reassembled at the output. This process is usually impractical, and one approximates the gain as something between G_0 and G_p. Often the approximation is poor and it is necessary to adjust the amplitudes and recompute the samples to avoid overloading or underloading the output. For this reason filters should be used sparingly.

The score record for FLT is

FLT I1, Ø, I2, I3, P_i, P_j

where P_i and P_j are two unused note parameters in which $Ø_{i-1}$ and $Ø_{i-1}$ are stored.

Composing Subroutines—PLF

Our tutorial discussion of what might be called the basics of sound generation is now complete. We are ready to take up compositional subroutines that will permit the generation of note parameters by the computer. These are some of the most interesting but difficult directions in which computer sound generation can be developed. Advanced applications point toward complete pieces composed by computer. However, long before these goals are achieved, PLF subroutines will be useful in saving the human composer from much routine work.

So far, for each note to be played, the composer has had to write a line of score starting with NØT.... PLF subroutines will now be developed which write these NØT records. Furthermore, one score record that evokes a PLF subroutine can generate many NØT's.

Although PLF programs can do other things besides compute NØT records, these records are of overriding importance and are the reason for creating PLF's. Moreover, Pass I itself is justified because it serves to contain the PLF subroutines.

Let us develop an example to demonstrate and teach the possibilities and practices of PLF programs. The example will allow storing a group of N notes in Pass I memory. A call to a PLF1, which we shall write, will insert these N notes anywhere in a composition and modify the notes by an arbitrary frequency shift, by an arbitrary tempo shift, and by specifying the instrument on which they will be played.

Figure 41 illustrates the use of PLF1. The first four score records store the four-note pattern in Pass I variable storage, using variables 10 through 43. Like the other passes, Pass I has a general storage array D(2000), which contains 2000 locations in the training orchestra. The

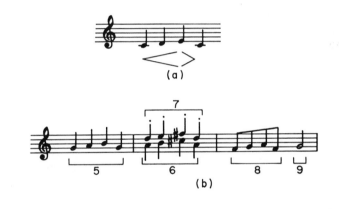

```
1   SV1 0 10 0 1 52 0 ;
2   SV1 0 20 1 1 56 .167 ;
3   SV1 0 30 2 1 60 .333 ;
4   SV1 0 40 3 1 56 0 ;
5   PLF 0 1 10 40 0 1 .583 4 ;
6   PLF 0 1 10 40 4 1 .750 4 ;
7   PLF 0 1 10 40 4 1 1.167 5 ;
8   PLF 0 1 10 40 8 .5 .417 4 ;
9   PLF 0 1 10 10 10 2 .583 4 ;
```

(c)

Fig. 41. PLF note-generating example: (a) pattern; (b) conventional score; (c) computer score.

PLF1 routine will assume that a note is described by four numbers

Starting time in seconds
Duration in seconds
Amplitude in decibels
Frequency in logarithmic units

in four successive D locations. Successive notes in a pattern will be separated by 10 locations in D, so that the first note goes into D(10), the second into D(20), etc., as is accomplished by the SV1 records.

The logarithmic frequency scale is introduced here. The composer will write scale numbers which are related to frequency by the equation

$$\text{Scale} = \log_2 \left(\frac{\text{frequency in hertz}}{262.0} \right)$$

This is probably the most useful scale for compositional algorithms. Middle C_{262} is 0, C_{512} is $+1$, etc.; the even-tempered half step is an increment of $\frac{1}{12}$. Thus

$$C_{262} = 0$$
$$C\# = .083$$
$$D = .167$$
$$D\# = .250$$
$$E = .333$$
$$F = .417$$
$$G = .583$$
$$G\# = .667$$
$$A = .750$$
$$A\# = .833$$
$$B = .917$$
$$C_{512} = 1.000$$

The even-tempered standard musical intervals are

$$\text{half step} = \tfrac{1}{12} = .083$$
$$\text{full step} = \tfrac{1}{6} = .167$$
$$\text{minor third} = \tfrac{1}{4} = .250$$
$$\text{major third} = \tfrac{1}{3} = .333$$
$$\text{fourth} = \tfrac{5}{12} = .417$$
$$\text{fifth} = \tfrac{7}{12} = .583$$

Frequency transposition can be done simply by adding a constant to the scale steps of a pattern. Multiplication corresponds to increasing or decreasing the size of the intervals in a pattern. Scales other than 12-tone can be represented with equal facility. The logarithmic scale is so powerful and appropriate that we will use it almost exclusively from here on.

In Fig. 41 score records 5 through 9 evoke the PLF subroutine that is to be presented. The P fields in these records have the following significance.

P1   calls a PLF subroutine

P2   is not used since action time has no importance in Pass I

P3   identifies the subroutine number (PLF1)

P4   gives the D location of the first note in the pattern

P5   gives the D location of the last note in the pattern

P6   gives the time in seconds at which the pattern should begin

P7   gives the duration scaling of the pattern; .5 = play at double speed; 2 = play at half speed

P8   gives the logarithmic interval to shift the frequency of the pattern. For example, P8 = .583 corresponds to shifting the theme up by a fifth

P9   gives the instrument number on which the pattern should be played

P1 through P3 have the same significance for all PLF routines. The rest of the P's depend entirely on the particular subroutine to be written.

The conventional score for the notes produced by records 5 through 9 is shown in Fig. 41 with the notes coming from a given record identified. Record 5 produces the first four notes in which the pattern is shifted up by a fifth. Records 6 and 7 produce two copies of the pattern playing in fourths. The upper voice is played on instrument 5 which is assumed to yield a staccato timbre. Record 8 plays the pattern at double speed. Record 9 plays the first note of the pattern at half speed.

In order to write a PLF program we will have to know something of the operation of Pass I. It reads the score records in the order in which they appear in the score. The SV1 records cause data to be stored in the D(2000) memory. A NØT record would simply cause the record to be sent on to Pass II. This is accomplished by placing the NØT data in the P(100) array and calling a communication routine WRITE1, which writes out the P array on a file that will later be read by Pass II. For bookkeeping purposes, the number of parameters in the record is kept in another Pass I location IP(1) and is automatically written out by WRITE1. The function of the PLF routine is to generate NØT records and to write them out exactly as Pass I would have done with a record in the score.

How is the PLF routine brought into action? When Pass I reads a PLF score record it calls a subroutine PLFn, in which n is in P3. The rest of the data on the score record is in the P array where it can be used by the subroutine.

The annotated PLF1 routine to perform the computations we have described follows.

Text	Notes
SUBRØUTINE PLF1	1
CØMMØN IP, P, D	
DIMENSIØN IP(10), P(100), D(2000)	
NS = P(4)	2
NE = P(5)	
TS = P(6)	
DS = P(7)	
FS = P(8)	
IP(1) = 6	3
P(1) = 1.0	4
P(3) = P(9)	5
DØ 100 I = NS, NE, 10	6
P(2) = TS + DS * D(I)	7
P(4) = DS * D(I + 1)	8
P(5) = D(I + 2)	9
P(6) = (2.0 ** (D(I + 3) + FS)) * 262.0	10
CALL WRITE1(10)	11
100 CØNTINUE	
RETURN	
END	

Notes

1. This CØMMØN and DIMENSIØN statement locates the three essential arrays, IP, P, and D for PLF1. The Pass I definition of these arrays must agree with the definition in the subroutine.
2. These statements take parameters P4–P8 from the PLF data record and store them in the PLF subroutine. Since the P(100) array will be used to output NØT records, the PLF parameters must be removed from it.
3. The word count of the NØT records is set at 6. We will assume that we are generating notes for an instrument of a type shown in Fig. 39. The six fields are

    P1 NØT
    P2 Action time in seconds

P3 Instrument number
P4 Duration in seconds
P5 Amplitude in decibels
P6 Note frequency in hertz

4. The programs convert all alphabetical symbols into numerical equivalents in the initial reading routine in Pass I. All subsequent processing is done on the numbers. The equivalence of NØT is 1.0, which is set by this statement.
5. This statement sets the instrument number into P(3). P(1) and P(3) are constant for all the notes in the pattern and hence can be set once at the beginning.
6. This DØ loop is executed once for each NØT in the pattern. The storage of the pattern in the D array is inherently defined by the loop, the first note beginning at D(NS), the last note beginning at D(NE), the notes being 10 locations apart.
7. This statement computes the starting time of the note as the PLF time shift TS, plus the duration scale DS, times the starting time relative to the beginning of the pattern D(I).
8. This statement computes the scaled duration of the note.
9. This statement transfers the amplitude of the note from the pattern to the P(100) array. No modification of amplitude is necessary.
10. This statement adds the frequency transposition FS to the pattern frequency $D(I + 3)$, and converts the sum from a logarithmic to a linear frequency scale in hertz.
11. This statement calls for writing out the completed NØT record.

In this example it is already possible to see many labor-saving advantages in PLF. Although the pattern is atypically short, 17 notes are produced by only five data records, far fewer than are needed to write a separate NØT record for each note.

Next let us discuss a slightly more complicated and considerably more interesting PLF routine. It takes the product of two themes, in a sense. Each note in the first theme is replaced by the entire second theme. The second theme is scaled for duration; its total duration exactly equals the duration of the note it replaces. The log frequencies of the second theme are increased by the log frequencies of the replaced note, so that the second theme is centered about each note of the first theme. Amplitudes are similarly treated. The process is reminiscent of some "theme and development" styles. The second theme can be considered an ornament applied to the first theme.

An example is shown in Fig. 42, where the first theme, the second theme, and the product are written in musical notation. Typically, theme 2 is short and compact in frequency range. However, this is not a requirement. We could also form the product

Theme 2 × theme 1

Our multiplication algorithm is not commutative, and

Theme 1 × theme 2 ≠ theme 2 × theme 1

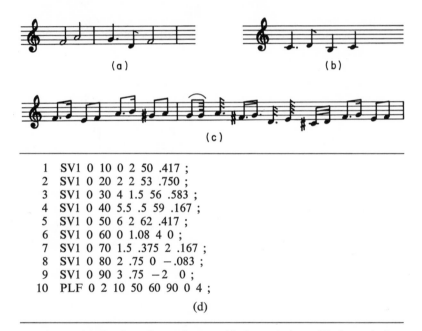

(a)

(b)

(c)

```
 1   SV1 0 10 0 2 50 .417 ;
 2   SV1 0 20 2 2 53 .750 ;
 3   SV1 0 30 4 1.5 56 .583 ;
 4   SV1 0 40 5.5 .5 59 .167 ;
 5   SV1 0 50 6 2 62 .417 ;
 6   SV1 0 60 0 1.08 4 0 ;
 7   SV1 0 70 1.5 .375 2 .167 ;
 8   SV1 0 80 2 .75 0 −.083 ;
 9   SV1 0 90 3 .75 −2  0 ;
10   PLF 0 2 10 50 60 90 0 4 ;
```

(d)

Fig. 42. Multiplication of two themes: (a) theme 1 times (b) theme 2 gives (c) product via PLF2; (d) computer score.

The score for the example is also shown in Fig. 42. Lines 1–5 define theme 1, lines 6–9 define theme 2, and line 10 calls PLF2 to generate the product. The calling sequence is

P4   D location of first note of first theme
P5   D location of last note of first theme
P6   D location of first note of second theme
P7   D location of last note of second theme
P8   Starting time of product theme
P9   Instrument number

We will assume that the D array arrangement and the instrument are the same as were used for PLF1.

The annotated FØRTRAN program follows.

Text	Notes
SUBRØUTINE PLF2	
CØMMØN IP, P, D	
DIMENSIØN IP(10), P(100), D(2000)	
NB1 = P(4)	1
NE1 = P(5)	
NB2 = P(6)	
NE2 = P(7)	
TS = P(8)	
IP(1) = 6	
P(1) = 1.0	
P(3) = P(9)	
DØ 101 I = NB1, NE1, 10	2
START = TS + D(I)	3
DS = D(I + 1)/(D(NE2) + D(NE2 + 1))	
DØ 100 J = NB2, NE2, 10	2
P(2) = START + DS * D(J)	4
P(4) = DS * D(J + 1)	
P(5) = D(J + 2) + D(I + 2)	
P(6) = (2.0 ** (D(J + 3) + D(I + 3)) * 262.0	
CALL WRITE1(10)	
100 CØNTINUE	
101 CØNTINUE	
RETURN	
END	

Notes

1. This group of statements moves the PLF parameters from the P(100) array into the subroutine and sets the unchanging parts of the NØT parameters in P(100) in preparation for writing NØT records.
2. The program contains two nested DØ loops. The outer loop is executed once for each note in theme 1, the inner DØ cycles for each note in theme 2.
3. These two statements compute the starting time shift and the duration scaling for a repetition of theme 2. START is the beginning time of a note in theme 1. DS is computed so that the last note in theme 2 will end at the ending time of the note in theme 1.
4. This and the following three statements compute the starting times, durations, amplitudes, and frequencies for the notes in theme 2

which are replacing a single note in theme 1. Amplitudes in decibels and frequencies on a logarithmic scale are simply added. Frequencies are converted to hertz.

These two examples give only a slight indication of the range of objectives that may be programmed with PLF routines. The routines are not limited to generating NØT records. They may also be used to manipulate the information stored in the D array of Pass I. A powerful application is a set of PLF routines, each of which effects a different transform on a set of notes stored in the D array. Since the result of each transform must be in the same form as its input, several transforms may be successively applied. Finally, a last PLF writes out the NØT records. A composition using these subroutines would consist of the description of some thematic material, plus a long sequence of PLF calls to manipulate this material.

The PLF routines provide one of the most exciting areas for further development in the entire Music V structure. Not only do they promise the most interesting possibilities, but they also offer the greatest challenges to the composer's creativity.

Compositional Functions

The note-generating subroutines that have just been demonstrated can be greatly strengthened by defining information in certain ways which we call compositional functions. Compositional functions can be used to provide a new language to describe sounds, called a graphic score. Although graphic scores can be used to represent the notes in a conventional score, the notation is completely different. It is more powerful in the sense that many sounds that are impossible to notate conventionally can be readily described by a graphic score. Moreover, in the synthesis of sounds, the graphic scores can be "read" easily by note-generating subroutines. This section can only lay the foundation for graphic scores, but further information is given in the references.

A compositional function is a function defined over an entire section of a composition. It is used to control some always present parameter such as loudness or tempo. Compositional functions should not be confused with the stored function used to describe waveshape or envelope. The stored functions are generated, stored, and used in Pass III. Compositional functions are described and used in the first two passes. Both their mode of description and their use differ from those of stored functions.

Metronome Function

Let us start by considering the metronome function which is built into Pass II and can be evoked if desired. So far, the starting times and durations of notes have been written in numbers which were interpreted as seconds. Thus a note

NØT 2 4 1 54 .167 ;

starts at 2 sec from the beginning of the section and lasts for 1 sec. With a metronome function, P2 and P4 are interpreted in beats; the note starts at the beginning of the second beat of the section and lasts for one beat. The relation between beats and seconds is given by the metronome function, which is in standard metronome marking of beats per minute. Thus, for example, if the metronome function is 180, the note would start $\frac{2}{3}$ sec from the beginning of the section and would last $\frac{1}{3}$ sec.

The metronome function need not be constant, but can change abruptly or gradually during a section to introduce accelerandos or retards. The operation can be illustrated by an example shown in Fig. 43.

The conventional score for 14 quarter notes lasting 14 beats is shown at the top, together with tempo marking. The NØT cards to encode this are as follows.

NØT	0	4	.8	60	0	;
NØT	1	4	.8	60	.167	;
NØT	2	4	.8	60	.333	;
NØT	3	4	.8	60	0	;
NØT	4	4	.8	60	0	;
NØT	5	4	.8	60	.167	;
NØT	6	4	.8	60	.333	;
NØT	7	4	.8	60	.417	;
NØT	8	4	.8	60	.583	;
NØT	9	4	.8	60	.750	;
NØT	10	4	.8	60	.917	;
NØT	11	4	.8	60	.583	;
NØT	12	4	.8	60	.583	;
NØT	13	4	.8	60	.750	;

The metronome function is evoked and is stored in Pass II variable storage by the records

SV2 0 50 0 60 4 60 8 120 11.9 120 12 30 14 30 ;
SV2 0 2 50 ;

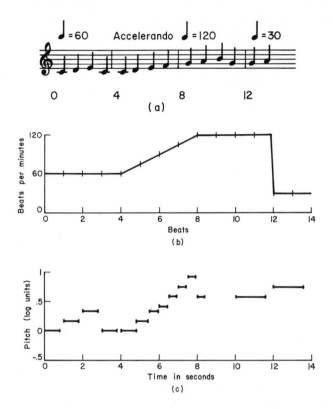

Fig. 43. Metronome function: (a) music score; (b) metronome marking function; (c) graphic score.

The first record describes the function, and P4 gives the initial abscissa (0), P5 the ordinate at that abscissa (60), P6 the next abscissa (4), P7 the next ordinate (60), etc. The abscissa is in beats and the ordinate in metronome marking—beats per minute. Successive points on the function are connected by straight lines, as shown in Fig. 43. As many segments as desired may be used by putting more points into the SV2 function. The abscissa points need not be uniformly arranged.

The second record tells the Pass II program that a metronome function is being used and that it starts in variable 50, that is to say, in G(50).

The graphic score in Fig. 43 shows the notes resulting from the metronome function being applied to the score. The pitch of each note, plotted against the time it occurs, is shown by the horizontal bars. Pitch is given on a logarithmic scale, $0 =$ middle C, $+1 = C_{512}$. Time is in seconds. Such a graphic score has proved to be an effective way of displaying many computer note sequences.

The first four notes, at a tempo of 60, occupy the first 4 sec. The second measure is played at an increasing tempo from 4 to 6.5 sec. The third measure at a tempo of 120 lasts from 6.5 to 8.5 sec. The last two notes, at a tempo of 30, go from 10 to 14 sec.

The computation relating metronome function to a note's starting time and duration consists in sampling the metronome function at the beginning of the note. These sampling points are indicated by ticks on the function. Thus the sixth note has a tempo value of 75. The duration and starting time of the note are defined as

$$\text{Duration} = \text{P4} \times \tfrac{60}{75} \text{ sec}$$
$$= .8 \times \tfrac{60}{75} = .64 \text{ sec}$$

and

$$\text{Starting time} = \text{starting time of previous note}$$
$$+ (\text{P2 of note} - \text{P2 of previous note}) \cdot \tfrac{60}{75}$$
$$= 4 + (5 - 4) \cdot \tfrac{60}{75} = 4.8 \text{ sec}$$

Because the metronome function for the 13th note is sampled at 12 beats, its value is 30, and a rather long silence occurs between the 12th and 13th notes. Such a silence is inherent in the algorithm. It is seldom objectionable; also such large changes in tempo seldom occur.

If several voices are playing simultaneously, the same metronome function is applied to all.

Metronome functions have proved to be powerful tools for inserting accelerandos and ritardandos. Without them, the calculation of starting times and durations of gradually changing note sequences can be very tedious. In addition, they enable the composer to write in terms of conveniently defined beats, rather than seconds, which often turn out to be unwieldy decimals.

A Note-Generating Subroutine and Graphic Score

The metronome function is built into Pass II. Let us now write a subroutine PLF3, which will generate a voice from a complete, if elementary, graphic score. A sample score is shown in Fig. 44. Four functions are used to describe the voice—duration, duty factor, pitch, and amplitude. All are functions of time, which in this example goes from 0 to 13 sec.

The duration function in Fig. 44a gives the time from the beginning of one note to the beginning of the following note. The first note starts

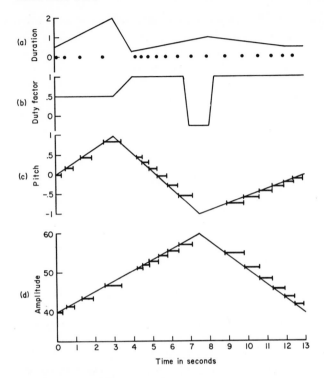

Fig. 44. Graphic score and resulting notes: (a) duration; (b) duty factor; (c) pitch; and (d) amplitude.

at t = 0, where the value of the duration function is .5 sec. The second note starts at .5 sec, where the value of the duration function is .8 sec; the third note starts at 1.3 sec (1.3 = .5 + .8), and so on. In other words, the duration function is sampled at the beginning of each note to obtain the interval to the beginning of the next note. The actual sampling times are shown as dots along the abscissa of Fig. 44a. Although there are more advanced ways of representing durations graphically, this representation is easy to program and is useful for a number of purposes.

The rhythm is represented by the duration function. The style of playing—legato or staccato—is represented by the duty-factor function, Fig. 44b, which gives the proportion of the interval between the starting times of successive notes that is occupied by sound. The first note has a duty factor of .5. Its length will be .25 sec (.5 duty factor × .5-sec interval to start of the second note). A duty factor of .25 produces an exceedingly staccato note sequence. A duty factor of 1 produces a smooth legato. A duty factor greater than 1 causes overlap of successive notes. Like the duration function, the duty-factor function is sampled. The duty factor for each note is the value of the duty-factor function at the starting time of the note. Duty-factor function will be somewhat arbitrarily used for one other purpose. A negative duty factor will indicate a rest—the note will be omitted entirely.

The pitch and amplitude functions, Fig. 44c and d, are also sampled at the starting time of each note to obtain pitch and amplitude. Pitch is written in our logarithm scale, $C_{262} = 0$, $C_{512} = 1$, etc. Amplitude is written in decibels. A graphic representation of the actual notes that are generated are shown as horizontal bars superimposed on the pitch and amplitude functions. Pitches can be read from the pitch scale, amplitudes from the amplitude scale, durations and starting times from the beginning and ending times of either the pitch or amplitude bars. Because of the sampling process, the left end of each bar starts on the pitch or amplitude function.

The functions shown graphically in Fig. 44 must be represented numerically in the computer memory in Pass I. The convention that represented the metronome function will again be employed; successive breakpoints will be given by their abscissa and ordinate values. The data will be stored in the Pass I D(2000) array by SV1 cards. Thus the duration, duty factor, pitch, and amplitude functions in Fig. 44 are described by the following four records

---

Duration: SV1 0 50 0 .5 3 2 4 .3 8 1 12 .5 13 .5 ;
Duty factor: SV1 0 65 0 .5 3 .5 4 1 6.7 1 7 −.25 8 −.25
                 8.3 1 13 1 ;
Pitch: SV1 0 85 0 0 3 1 7.5 −1 13 0 ;
Amplitude: SV1 0 95 0 40 7.5 60 13 40 ;

The functions start in D(50). The amount of memory occupied by a function depends on the number of breakpoints. Successive functions have been arbitrarily spaced by sufficient multiples of five so as not to overlap.

A FØRTRAN function CØN has been provided to read the graphic functions. The statement

Z = CØN (D, N, T)

sets Z equal to the value, at time T, of the function that starts at D(N).

Thus, for example,

Z = CØN (D, 95, 3.0)

would set Z equal to 48, which is the value of the amplitude function at 3 sec. The values are computed by interpolating a straight line between the breakpoints that surround T (0 and 7.5 in the specific example). CØN must search the D array to find these breakpoints. It is essential not to ask for values of the function outside the range of breakpoints that have been defined. Otherwise CØN may never terminate its search.

We can now write a subroutine PLF3 to generate notes from graphic scores. The data record to call this routine is

PLF 0 3 TS END NA NP NDR NDF IN ;

where TS is a time shift giving the starting time of the sequence of notes to be produced by PLF3; END is the duration of the sequence; NA, NP, NDR, and NDF give the starting points in the D array of the amplitude, pitch, duration, and duty-factor functions, respectively. IN gives the instrument number.

An example to produce the notes shown in Fig. 44 is:

PLF 0 3 0 13 95 85 50 65 4 ;

We shall assume that the program writes out records in the form (which has been used frequently)

NØT TS IN D AMP PITCH ;

where AMP and PITCH are in decibels and log units.

The annotated PLF3 subroutine follows.

Text	Notes
SUBRØUTINE PLF3	
CØMMØN IP, P, D	
DIMENSIØN IP(10), P(100), D(2000)	
TS = P(4)	
END = P(5)	1
NA = P(6)	
NP = P(7)	
NDR = P(8)	
NDF = P(9)	
P(1) = 1.0	2
P(3) = P(10)	
IP(1) = 6	
T = 0.0	3

```
100   DR = CØN(D, NDR, T)                        4
      IF(T + DR − END) 101, 101, 104             5
101   P(2) = T + TS                              6
      P(4) = DR * CØN(D, NDF, T)                 7
      IF(P(4)) 103, 103, 102                     8
102   P(5) = CØN(D, NA, T)                       9
      P(6) = CØN(D, NP, T)
      CALL WRITE1(10)
103   T = T + DR                                 10
      GØ TØ 100                                  11
104   RETURN
      END
```

Notes

1. These statements extract the essential information for the PLF3 from the P array.
2. These statements set the constant parts of the P array in preparation for writing out NØT records, and they set the word count.
3. T is the starting time of the next note to be generated (not including the time shift TS). It is set initially at zero and computed as a running variable and is increased by the interval between successive notes after each note is generated. T is also the variable used to specify abscissa values in CØN.
4. DR is the interval between successive notes as obtained by CØN from the duration function.
5. This statement checks to see whether the starting time of the next note is greater than the ending time, END. If so, the current note is not generated and PLF3 is terminated.
6. The time shift TS is added to T to obtain the starting time of the note.
7. The duration of the note is computed as the interval times the duty factor.
8. This statement checks for a rest. If the duration is zero or negative, owing to a zero or negative duty factor, no NØT is written out and the program proceeds to the next note.
9. These statements compute the rest of the NØT parameters and write out the NØT record.
10. This statement adds T to the starting time of the next note.
11. This statement transfers control in order to generate the next note.

Several features of the operation of PLF3 may be pointed out in Fig. 44. The first four notes are staccato, having large silences between notes. The next six notes are legato, with no silent intervals between notes. Two possible notes have been omitted to form a rest.

In terms of the number of notes generated, PLF3 is very efficient. One PLF3 call produced 16 notes. It could just as well have produced 1600. In contrast to conventional scores, the notation for duration has the advantage that a second's worth of fast notes requires no more effort to describe than a second's worth of slow notes. Also ritardandos and accelerandos are easy to describe by lines with increasing or decreasing slopes, as illustrated from 4 to 8 and from 8 to 13 sec. Such tempo changes can have striking acoustical effect.

Pass II Subroutines—PLS Pitch-Quantizing Example

To complete the discussion of NØT-generating subroutines and note-manipulating subroutines, we will write one second-pass subroutine. Pass II routines cannot be used to generate additional notes since all the NØT records have been carefully sorted in increasing order of action times, and the addition of more NØT records would disrupt the ordering. However, PLS routines can change the values of note parameters (except action times). Since notes of all voices are sorted together, it is convenient for PLS to embody relations involving several voices at a particular time. For example, PLS could well be used to adjust the pitch intervals between voices.

We will not attempt quite as complicated an example as interval control. Instead we will control the pitches of a single voice so that they fall exactly on the steps of a previously specified scale. Such a process makes sense when applied to the output of the PLF3 routine that was presented in the preceding section. The pitches so generated are samples of a continuous pitch function and can fall anywhere. Sometimes it is desirable to limit the possible pitches to a prespecified set or scale. The scale need not correspond to any known or standard musical scale, such as a just scale or a 12-tone scale. An octave can be divided into any number of intervals; the intervals can be even tempered (equal) or unequal in size.

Figure 45 gives an example of the output of the routine to be written. It is applied to the notes generated by the PLF3 program. The pitch function and notes from Fig. 44 have been redrawn in Fig. 45. For the scale the octave is divided into five equal intervals, as shown in Fig. 45. Since pitch is in logarithmic units, these units correspond to equal musical intervals. The PLS routine will adjust the pitches of the notes generated by PLS to the closest scale step. The pitches generated by

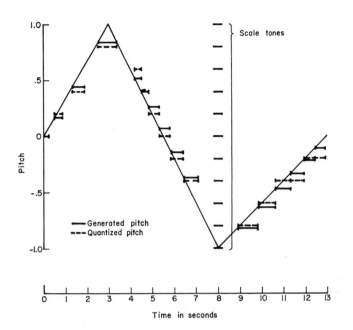

Fig. 45. Pitch quantizing by a PLS routine.

PLF are shown as solid horizontal bars, and the adjusted pitches are shown as dashed bars. The adjustment may be either up or down, depending on which scale step is closest. The process of adjustment is called pitch quantizing.

Note that the first and sixth notes happened to fall exactly on a scale step and require no quantizing. Also the last two pairs of notes become pairs of repeated notes as a result of quantizing. Quantizing tends to produce repeated notes if the scale steps are large and the change in pitch between successive notes is small.

In order to write a PLS routine, it is necessary to understand a few details of the operation of Pass II. All the data records in a section are read into a large array D(10,000), 10,000 locations long in the training orchestra. An array I(1000) is computed by sorting so that

$I(1)$ = the address in D of the beginning of "first" data record where "first" means smallest action time

$I(2)$ = the address in D of the beginning of "second" data record

etc.

For example if the thirteenth data record is

NØT 19 2 4 60 .167 ;

and is stored starting at D(109), then

I(13) = 109

and

D(109) = 6   (Word count)
D(110) = 1   (NØT ≡ 1)
D(111) = 19
D(112) = 2
D(113) = 4
D(114) = 60
D(115) = .167

After I(1000) is computed, the program goes through the data records in order of increasing action times, executing any PLS routines, storing any SV2 data in the G(1000) Pass II data array, and writing out NØT records with the aid of the CØNVT subroutine.

A PLS function can modify any NØT records with action times greater than the action time of the PLS function. It cannot affect NØT records with action times less than the PLS function, since these will already have been written before PLS is executed. The Pass II memory G(1000) will contain the numbers from any SV2 cards with action times less than the action time on the PLS function; it will not contain any data from SV2 cards whose action times are greater than on the PLS function.

The scale will be stored in Pass II memory by a SV2 statement giving the number of steps in the scale, followed by the pitches of these steps. Thus the scale used in Fig. 45 is inserted in the memory by the record

SV2 0 100 11 −1 −.8 −.6 −.4 −.2 0 .2 .4 .6 .8 1 ;

These data will go into G memory at time 0.

The PLS1 function will be called at action time 0 by the statement

PLS 0 1 100;

where P3 = 1 indicates PLS1 and the 100 gives the starting point of the scale in the G array.

An annotated program to carry out the pitch quantizing follows.

	Text	Notes

	SUBRØUTINE PLS1	
	CØMMØN IP, P, G, I, T, D	1
	DIMENSIØN IP(10), P(100), G(1000), I(1000),	
	T(1000), D(10,000)	
	I1 = IP(2)	2
	IN = IP(3)	3
	NQ = D(I1 + 4)	4
	NB = NQ + 1	
	NL = NQ + IFIX(G(NQ))	
	DØ 103 J = 1, IN	5
	ID = I(J)	
	IF(D(ID + 1) − 1.0) 103, 100, 103	6
100	FREQ = D(ID + 6)	7
	MIN = 1,000,000.0	8
	DØ 102 K = NB, NL	
	IF(ABS(FREQ − G(K)) − MIN) 101, 102, 102	
101	MIN = ABS(FREQ − G(K))	
	QFREQ = G(K)	
102	CØNTINUE	
	D(ID + 6) = QFREQ	9
103	CØNTINUE	
	RETURN	
	END	

Notes

1. This common statement and the subsequent dimension statement describe the main data arrays in Pass II and must agree with the corresponding statements in the Pass II main program. IP gives certain miscellaneous constants, P is the communication array from which data records are read and written, G is general variable storage, I indexes the D array in action-time order, T contains action times and is primarily used in the sorting process, D contains the data records.

2. When PLS is called, IP(2) contains the address in the D array at which the PLS data record is located. In this case if

$$IP(2) = 27$$

then

$$D(27) = \quad 4 \quad \text{(Word count)}$$
$$D(28) = \quad 10 \quad (PLS \equiv 10)$$
$$D(29) = \quad 0$$
$$D(30) = \quad 1$$
$$D(31) = 100$$

3. IP(3) contains the number of data records in D. The main DØ loop in the PLS routine will examine I(J) for J = 1 to IP(3).
4. This and the subsequent two statements determine NB and NL as the first and last locations of the scale description in the G array. A DØ loop will test these locations.
5. The main DØ loop examines all data statements in order of ascending action times. ID in the subsequent statement is the D address of the data statement.
6. This statement checks to see if the data statement is a NØT record. If not, it is skipped; if so, the pitch variable P6 is quantized.
7. FREQ is set equal to the pitch P6.
8. This and the subsequent statements to 102 determine the scale step that is closest to FREQ. MIN is initially set to a very large value. The absolute value of (FREQ − each scale step) is compared with MIN and if it is smaller than MIN, MIN is reset to that value. In this way MIN ends being the smallest interval and QFREQ ends being the closest frequency.
9. This statement resets the pitch D(ID + 6) to the closest scale step.

The PLS routines tend to be both longer and logically more complicated than the PLF routines. The steps in the example just discussed are typical. Actually, they were not all necessary for the problem at hand. The pitches could have been quantized by the PLF routine as they were generated. Even if the quantizing were done in Pass II, it would not have been necessary to go through the D array in order of action times. However, for slightly more complicated operations, such as quantizing the intervals between voices, all the Pass II steps are essential.

Another simplification in the program consists in writing out the scale for all the octaves in which it is to be used. In many cases, only one octave is written out; the actual pitches are translated to this octave before being quantized; and the quantized pitches are translated back to their original octave. The possibilities open to the composer are almost endless.

Interactions Between Instruments

The final process to be considered in this chapter involves interactions between instruments. The desirability for such interactions arises from the limitations of the "note concept," which defines sounds as having starting and ending times. Sometimes it is desirable to produce continuous sounds that change from time to time in controlled ways. As we shall show, this can be done by using the output of an instrument as an input to another instrument. The first instrument is degenerate in the sense that it produces no acoustic output. Instead it plays a series of notes that generate a long and frequently changing modulation function for the second instrument. The second instrument may play only a single long note whose sound is varied by the parameter supplied by the first instrument.

A typical and important use of interactions is amplitude control to produce swells and diminuendos as notated on the conventional score in Fig. 46. Such a modulation is unwieldy to program with the apparatus previously described. Although we can draw continuous amplitude

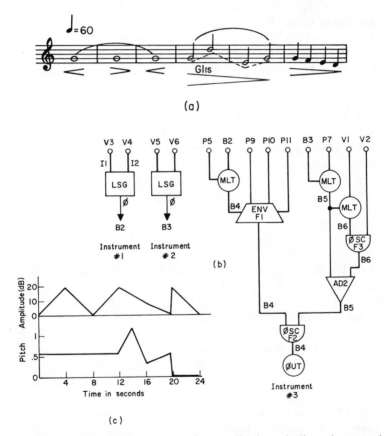

Fig. 46. Interconnected instruments for amplitude and glissando control: (a) musical score; (b) block diagrams of instruments; (c) continuous control functions.

functions, as is done in Fig. 44, these are sampled at the beginning of each note and that amplitude is held constant for the duration of the note; this effect is clearly not the desired objective of Fig. 46. Furthermore, since the inputs to instruments are set at the beginning of each note, the sampling effect is hard to avoid. In Fig. 46a, measures 4 and 5 also call for a combination of glissando with amplitude variation. The last measure applies a continuously changing amplitude control to a sequence of notes. As an example of interacting instruments, we shall produce these effects.

The apparatus for interactions is the input–output blocks B1–B10, which are shared by all instruments. The output of instrument A may be left in a block for subsequent use by instrument B. This requires that A be computed before B. Pass III computes the instruments in order of their numbers,[3] any that are #1 first, then any that are #2, and so forth. Hence by making A a lower numbered instrument than B, the proper order can be guaranteed. An additional requirement is that the block used for communication cannot be used for other purposes which would overwrite the output of A before B uses it. Also, in contrast to most instruments, A can generate only one voice at a time.

A special unit generator LSG, which rapidly computes functions formed from straight-line segments, is useful in instruments that generate control functions. Two such generators are used for instruments 1 and 2 in Fig. 46 to produce amplitude- and frequency-control signals, respectively. The operation of LSG is simply

$$I1_i = I1_i + I2_i$$
$$\emptyset_i = I1_i$$

or in other words I1 is incremented by I2 for each sample and $\emptyset$ is equal to I1. Because only addition is involved, the process is rapid. I1 will be set to a desired initial value and I2 to the slope of a linear function that starts at I1. I1 and I2 can be reset at any time, thus changing the value of $\emptyset$ and the slope abruptly. In instrument #1, Pass III variables 3 and 4 are used for I1 and I2. These will be set with SV3 records which are generated by a Pass I subroutine PLF4 to achieve a particular amplitude-control function. Instrument #2 produces the same effect for pitch. The outputs of instruments 1 and 2 are put in blocks B2 and B3 where they form inputs to instrument 3.

Instrument 3 is a modification of the envelope instrument which was

---

[3] As of February 21, 1968, this feature was not yet programmed in Music V. However, it seems both desirable and easy to insert.

developed in Fig. 39, and it uses the CØNVT function for that instrument. The additional amplitude function B2 is multiplied by the normal amplitude input P5. The continuous amplitude-control function is written in decibels (as shown in Fig. 46c), and B2 is the exponential transformation

$$B2 = 10 ** \left(\frac{\text{continuous amplitude function}}{20} \right)$$

Thus, the decibels of the normal amplitude function and the continuous function are additive. If the continuous function is 10 dB and the normal function is 50 dB, the resulting sound will be at 60 dB.

The normal frequency input P7 is multiplied by the additional frequency-control function B3. The continuous pitch function (also shown in Fig. 46c) will be written in our standard logarithmic scale, and B3 will be the exponential transformation

$$B3 = 2 ** \text{continuous pitch function}$$

Thus a continuous pitch function of 0 produces no change in pitch, a continuous pitch function of 1 produces a one-octave upward shift, and so forth. The computation of V3–V6 to achieve both the exponential conversions and the proper increments will be done by a PLF4 subroutine.

Input V1 specifies the proportion of frequency shift in the vibrato, proportionality being controlled by a multiplier. Such Pass III multiplication is essential rather than multiplication by the CØNVT function, because frequency can vary over a note.

The annotated PLF4 program is given below. The pitch and amplitude functions will be stored as Pass I variables in the usual notation. The functions shown in Fig. 46c are stored by the statements

    SV1 0 50 0 0 4 20 8 0 12 20 19.99 0 20 20 24 0 ;
    SV1 0 70 0 .583 12 .583 14 1.167 16 .333 19.99 .583 20 0
      24 0 ;

The calling record for PLF4 is

    PLF 0 4 TS END FA FP ;

where TS is the starting time of the control functions, END is the duration of the control functions, FA is the starting variable of the amplitude function, and FP is the starting variable of the pitch function. For the example

    PLF 0 4 0 24 50 70 ;

is the specific calling record.

PLF4 generates a sequence of SV3 records to form the inputs to instruments 1 and 2, and generates two NØT records to activate these instruments from 0 to 24 sec.

Text	Notes

```
      SUBRØUTINE PLF4
      CØMMØN IP, P, D
      DIMENSION IP(10), P(100), D(2000)
      TS = P(4)                                              1
      END = P(5)
      NA = P(6)
      NP = P(7)
      I = NA                                                 2
      IP(1) = 5
      P(1) = 4.0
      P(3) = 3.0
100   P(4) = 10.0 ** (D(I + 1)/20.0)                         3
      P(5) = (10.0 ** (D(I + 3)/20.0) − P(4))/((D(I + 2)
                                        − D(I)) * D(4))
      P(2) = TS + D(I)                                       4
      CALL WRITE1(10)
      IF (D(I + 2) − END) 101, 102, 102                      5
101   I = I + 2                                              6
      GØ TØ 100
102   I = NP
      P(3) = 5.0
103   P(4) = 2.0 ** D(I + 1)
      P(5) = ((2.0 ** D(I + 3) − P(4))/((D(I + 2)
                                    − D(I)) * D(4))
      P(2) = TS + D(I)
      CALL WRITE1(10)
      IF(D(I + 2) − END) 104, 105, 105
104   I = I + 2
      GØ TØ 103
105   IP(1) = 4                                              8
      P(1) = 1.0
      P(2) = TS
      P(3) = 1.0
      P(4) = END
      CALL WRITE1(10)
      P(3) = 2.0
      CALL WRITE1(10)
      RETURN
      END
```

Notes
1. These statements extract the essential information for PLF4 from the P array.
2. These statements prepare to write SV3 records for V3 and V4. P(1) is 4 for SV3. P(3) = 3.0 designates V3 as the first variable. One pair of V3 and V4 values will be written for each segment of the amplitude function. I = NA will set the initial value of the equations starting at 100 for the first segment.
3. This and the subsequent line calculate the initial value and slope for the first segment. The slope is in units per sample. D(4) is the sampling rate.
4. The time of the SV3 card is the beginning time of the first segment plus TS.
5. This statement terminates the amplitude function at the end of the current segment if $D(I + 2) \geq$ END.
6. I is incremented by 2 and control is transferred to 100 to continue with the next segment.
7. These statements write out SV3 records for variables 5 and 6 to produce the pitch control. The process is exactly analogous to amplitude control.
8. The rest of the program writes out two NØT records

> NØT TS 1 END
> NØT TS 2 END

that play two notes on instruments 1 and 2 which start at TS and have duration END.

The score records to produce the Fig. 46 output are given below. The definition of the instruments and the Pass III stored functions are omitted since they are completely standard.

```
SV1 0 50 0 0 4 20 8 0 12 20 19.99 0 20 20 24 0 ;
SV1 0 70 0 .583 12 .583 14 1.167 16 .333 19.99 .583 20 0
   24 0 ;
PLF 0 4 0 24 50 70 ;
NØT 0 3 11.8 40 262 ;
NØT 12 3 7.8 40 262 ;
NØT 20 3 .8 40 392 ;
NØT 21 3 .8 40 349 ;
NØT 22 3 .8 40 330 ;
NØT 23 3 .8 40 294 ;
```

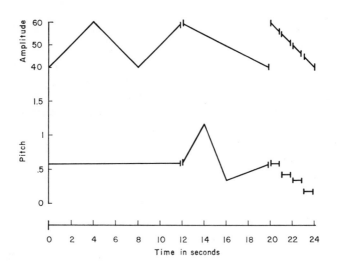

Fig. 47. Graphic score with continuous changes in amplitude and pitch.

The graphic score of the resulting sound is shown in Fig. 47. Beginnings and ends of individual notes are indicated by short vertical bars on the amplitude and pitch curves. An attack or decay will be produced by the envelope generator at these times. Amplitude and pitch changes occur continuously and independently of note boundaries.

Parting Exhortations to the Student

The tutorial examples are now complete. However, the student's task—harnessing the computer to his objectives—has just begun. A mere reading of the examples is not sufficient to master their content. The examples are a far from complete description of the Music V program; the Music V program as written will produce only a fraction of the wanted and achievable computer sounds.

Programming skills come only with practice. The problems accompanying this chapter provide some possibilities for practice. Their solution by the student is greatly recommended. If limited time forces a choice between reading the chapter and working the problems, working the problems is to be preferred.

Most of the problems are based on the material given in the chapter. In some cases, more details about the Music V program must be obtained. These can be found in the Music V Handbook which forms the next part of this book. The handbook is intended to be a complete description of the program, arranged and indexed for references. Information about Music V that has been given in this chapter is also presented in the handbook, and is usually easier to find there. The student should become accustomed to answering his questions from the handbook as soon as possible.

Although it is not necessary to read the entire handbook to make use of its information, anyone who plans to make extensive use of Music V should read the sections describing the operations of the various parts of the programs. Detailed block diagrams as well as verbal descriptions of operations are included. Reading the handbook is a helpful preparation for reading the programs themselves.

Music V is written almost entirely in FØRTRAN. Consequently, it is practical to read the programs and understand their operation. Such understanding is essential if major modifications of the programs are to be made. The advanced user will want to make such modifications; Music V was written with this objective in mind. Hence the student's final teacher, and the final arbiter of questions about the operation of Music V, is the programs. Such is the nature of computer programs.

Annotated References by Subject

Computers in General
J. Bernstein, *The Analytical Engine* (Random House, New York, 1964). A non-mathematical and elementary introduction to computers and what they can do.
A. Hassitt, *Computer Programming and Computer Systems* (Academic Press, New York, 1967). A discussion of programming from an elementary to an advanced viewpoint.

Fortran Programming
S. C. Plumb, *Introduction to Fortran* (McGraw-Hill, New York, 1964).
E. I. Organick, *Fortran IV Primer* (Addison-Wesley, Reading, Mass., 1966).
S. V. Pollack, *A Guide to Fortran IV* (Columbia University Press, New York, 1965).
These are three self-instructional texts that teach Fortran.

Graphic Scores
M. V. Mathews and L. Rosler, "Graphic Scores," *Perspectives of New Music 6*, No. 2 (1968). A detailed article illustrating one technique for composing with the aid of a computer.

Problems for Chapter 2

Parameters of Training Orchestra
      Sampling rate—20,000 Hz
      Function block length—512
      Number of functions—10

Range of functions——1 < F < +1
I-Ø block length—512
Number of I-Ø blocks—10
Range of unit generator inputs and outputs——2047 to +2047
Maximum number of note parameters—30
Number of Pass III variables—200
Maximum number of voices—30
Pass II G array length—1000
Pass I D array length—2000

Even-Tempered Scale

Note	Frequency in hertz	Logarithmic pitch
C	262	0
C#	277	.083
D	294	.167
D#	311	.250
E	330	.333
F	349	.417
F#	370	.500
G	392	.583
G#	415	.667
A	440	.750
A#	466	.833
B	494	.917

Introductory Score-Writing Problem

1. Using the orchestra defined in Fig. 27 write the computer score for the following conventional score.

Assume that in amplitude, p ≈ 50, mf ≈ 150, and f ≈ 500. Assume that staccato notes sound for .5 the nominal time occupied by the note (for example, a staccato quarter note at a tempo of 120 would sound for .25 sec). Legato notes sound for .8 of their nominal time, and slurred notes for 1.1 of their nominal time. (Remember that a Music V instrument can play more than one note at a time. The limit in the training orchestra is 30 simultaneous voices.)

Simple Unit Generators

2. Write out the samples $F_n(j)$ $j = 0 \ldots 511$ for the following stored functions. To shorten your answers, use ... to indicate a sequence of identical samples.

(a) F4, a symmetrical square wave with amplitude $+1$ or -1

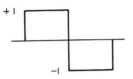

(b) F5, a triple pulse wave as shown

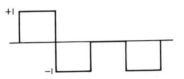

(c) F6, a sine wave of peak amplitude 1 (write only the first 20 samples)

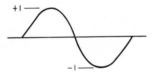

(d) F7, an attack function with shape

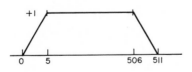

3. For an oscillator with
   I1 = 500
   I2 = 50.35
and a function F1

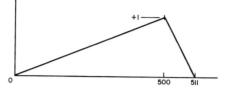

calculate S_i, $[S_i]_{\text{Mod } 511}$, $F([S_i]_{\text{Mod } 511})$

and $\emptyset_i$ for $i = 0\ldots15$

Assume $[S_i]_{\text{Mod } 511}$ is rounded to the next lower integer in looking up values of F1. Calculate the truncation error in $\emptyset_i$ due to rounding for $i = 0\ldots15$.

4. Instrument 1 consists of only one oscillator

ØSC P5 P6 B2 F4 P30 ;

where F4 is the symmetrical square wave defined in problem 2a. Write the samples B2(1)...B2(20) generated by the following notes

(a) NØT 0 1 .001 1000 250 ;
(b) NØT .002 1 .001 1000 50 ;
(c) NØT .004 1 .001 500 128.3 ;
(d) NØT .006 1 .001 1000 600 ;
(e) The numerical frequency of the last note is

$$\frac{600}{511} \cdot 20{,}000 = 23{,}500 \text{ Hz}$$

This frequency is much greater than half the sampling rate. What is the apparent period of B2(1)...B2(20)? This period (about 6 samples) results from foldover.

5. Instrument 1 shown in Fig. 27 uses the symmetrical square wave of problem 2a for its stored function. Write the output samples $S_0, S_1, \ldots, S_{60,000}$ resulting from the following score. Abbreviate your answer by designating blocks of zero samples by ...

NØT 0 1 .0005 1000 60 ;
NØT .5 1 .0006 500 200 ;
NØT 1 1 .0002 100 10 ;
NØT 2 1 .001 500 70 ;
NØT 2.0002 1 .0004 500 100 ;

6. Instrument 2 shown below uses F4 function of problem 2a. It plays the note

NØT 0 2 .001 500 80 3 100 ;

Plot the samples

B2(1)...B2(20)
B3(1)...B3(20)
B4(1)...B4(20)

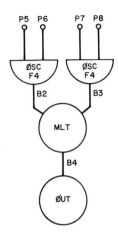

Instrument 2

Simple Instruments

7. Score the instrument diagrammed here.

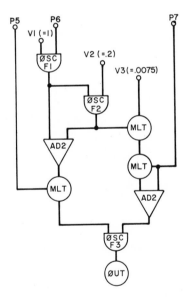

(a) What do P5, P6, and P7 control?
(b) What is the % vibrato?
(c) % amplitude variation?
(d) What is the rate of vibrato?

(e) Write score records for F1, an attack and decay function; F2, a vibrato function; and F3, a modified square-wave waveform.

(f) Write the score for the following passage

8. Diagram, score, and write functions and a note for an instrument that has attack and decay in amplitude and a frequency attack. The frequency of each note should start 10% low and rise linearly to the final frequency of the note within the first 10% of the note's duration.

9. Diagram and score an instrument with attack and decay in amplitude, with vibrato, and with attack and decay on the vibrato.

10. Diagram an instrument that uses four ØSC's to change the waveform of a note as a function of both amplitude and frequency. The composition of the output waveform should be

$$A \cdot [\{1000 - f\}\{(1 - A)ØSC_1 + A \cdot ØSC_2\}$$
$$+ \{f\}\{(1 - A)ØSC_3 + A \cdot ØSC_4\}]$$

where A is an amplitude control going from 0 to 1 and f is frequency in hertz.

CØNVT Functions

11. Write a CØNVT function for the instrument shown in Fig. 32 which will process a note record of the form

NØT T 2 D A F ;

where A is amplitude in decibels and F is frequency in hertz. V50 is the proportion of vibrato. For each NØT record, CØNVT should write out three records to produce a three-note chord, the highest voice having a frequency of A Hz, the middle voice A/2 Hz, and the lowest voice A/4 Hz.

12. Write a CØNVT function for the instrument shown in Fig. 33 which reads a NØT record of the form

NØT T 3 D A_1 A_2 ... A_n Freq

where A_1 ... A_n is a sequence of amplitudes in decibels and Freq is frequency in hertz. The CØNVT function outputs n + 1 successive notes of equal duration, whose total duration is D. The first note starts at amplitude 0 (linear scale) and ends at A_1(dB), the second goes from A_1 to A_2, ..., the last goes from A_n(dB) to 0 (linear scale).

Additional Unit Generators

13. Design an instrument with an amplitude-modulated band-pass noise having a bandwidth equal to $\frac{1}{4}$ the center frequency of the noise band, and a noise band whose center frequency changes linearly from an initial to a final frequency during each note.

14. Design an instrument having a random amplitude variation of $\pm 50\%$ of the average amplitude and a low-pass spectrum going from 0 to 15 Hz.

15. Design an instrument producing a band-pass noise by both frequency and amplitude modulation. Have the center frequency of the noise band controlled by P7 and the (bandwidth/center frequency) ratio by P8.

16. Write a CØNVT function for the instrument shown in Fig. 39 which will generate notes with an attack time of .1 sec and a decay time of .2 sec, provided the note duration is greater than .3 sec. The steady-state time should be (duration $-$ .3) sec. For notes of duration between .2 and .3 sec, the attack time should be .1 sec and the decay time (duration $-$ .1) sec. Any durations less than .2 sec should be increased to .2 sec.

17. Compute I2 and I3 for filters with a center frequency of 500 Hz and bandwidths of 2 Hz, 10 Hz, 50 Hz, and 260 Hz. What is the dc gain of these filters? What is the peak frequency gain? What is the maximum input signal that will not cause the output to exceed 2048?

Composing Subroutines

18. Write a set of PLF routines that will process note data in Pass I memory. Assume that the note data are stored in the Pass I D array in the manner used for the Fig. 41 example, and that notes will be written for the instrument shown in Fig. 39. Write the following subroutines:

(a) PLF1 rewrites n notes in the D array, multiplying all logarithmic pitch intervals by S, adding a constant K to the logarithmic pitch intervals, and changing the tempo by a factor T.

(b) PLF2 substitutes a new note for note n in the array.

(c) PLF3 makes a copy of n notes starting at $D(m)$ and stores the copied notes at $D(p)$, overwriting anything that was previously at $D(p)$.

(d) PLF4 divides each of n notes starting at $D(m)$ into k notes of equal length whose total duration equals that of the note they replace. The new notes are written starting at $D(p)$.

(e) PLF5 writes NØT records for n notes starting at $D(m)$. The starting times of all notes are shifted by T sec.

Use these subroutines to compute a composition.

Graphic Scores

19. Write a subroutine PLF1 that will generate pitch and amplitude functions as the computed functions

$$\text{Pitch}(t) = f_1(t) * f_2(t) + f_3(t) * f_4(t)$$
$$\text{Amplitude}(t) = f_5(t) * f_6(t) + f_7(t) * f_8(t)$$

where $f_1(t)$ through $f_8(t)$ are functions stored in the D array. Compute the starting and stopping times of notes as the positive-going zero crossings and the negative-going zero crossings, respectively, of a function

$$\text{Notes}(t) = f_9(t) * f_{10}(t) + (1 - f_9(t)) * f_{12}(t)$$

where $f_9(t)$, $f_{10}(t)$, $f_{12}(t)$ are stored in the D array. Let $f_{10}(t)$ and $f_{12}(t)$ correspond to the rhythmic sequence of two well-known melodies. What notes will be generated when $f_9(t) = 1$?; when $f_9(t) = 0$?; when $f_9(t)$ has some intermediate value? Follow the general procedures used in the Fig. 44 example.

Pitch Quantizing

20. Write PLS1, a pitch-quantizing routine which will quantize a voice for instrument 1 into the closest note in the C major scale. Assume that voices for instruments 2 and 3 produce notes in synchrony with instrument 1. Adjust these voices to harmonize instrument 1 according to the following rules.

(a) Harmonize C and E with the chord CEG.
(b) Harmonize F and A with the chord FAC.
(c) Harmonize B and D with GBD.
(d) Harmonize G with CEG if it starts on a multiple of four beats and with GED if it starts on any other beat.

Use a minimum adjustment of the other voices to achieve these chords.

Interconnected Instruments

21. Define an orchestra and an appropriate CØNVT function so that the output of an instrument is the sum of two ØSC's, the proportion of each being determined by two separate instruments I1 and I2. The proportion will change continuously and frequently during the course of the notes to add interest to the sound quality. Use LSG unit generators and follow the general procedures of the Fig. 46 example.

3 Music V Manual

M. V. Mathews, Joan E. Miller,
F. R. Moore, and J. C. Risset

3 Music V Manual

1. Introduction

This chapter contains a detailed description of the operation and structure of the Music V program. It provides reference material for users of Music V and source material for those who desire intimate knowledge of a sound-generating program in order to write their own.

Music V is the direct descendant of Music IV, a program that was widely used for five years and has been described in the literature.[1] Music V had to be rewritten to change from a second to a third generation computer (the IBM 7094 to the GE 645). However, in the process certain improvements were made, especially changes that made the program more easily adapted to other computers. It may be helpful to list these changes for the benefit of users of Music IV.

Principal Differences between Music IV and Music V

1. Music V is written almost entirely in FØRTRAN IV; it is much easier to use on a wide variety of computers. In addition, the FØRTRAN programs have been written so as to be easily modifiable to accommodate the different memory sizes and different word lengths of various computers.

---

[1] See Annotated References at end of chapter.

115

Despite being written in FØRTRAN, Music V is potentially as fast as Music IV. This potentiality can be achieved by writing the inner loops for certain computations (the unit generators) in basic machine language. Such programs are, of course, specific to a given computer, but at most only a few hundred instructions are involved.

FØRTRAN unit generators can be intermixed with basic machine-language generators. Initially, the program can be operated entirely with FØRTRAN generators. Gradually, the most frequently used generators can be coded in machine language. Exotic and infrequently used generators may remain in FØRTRAN at little cost. New generators can easily be added in FØRTRAN.

2. Instruments are defined as part of the score rather than in a separate program. (In Music IV the orchestra was assembled by the BE FAP assembly program.) In this way the entire composition—notes and timbres—is specified in a single document, the score. In addition, instruments may be redefined or changed at any point in the score.

3. A given instrument may play any number of voices simultaneously. Only one instrument of a given type need be defined; the composer no longer need worry about losing notes that overlap in time on an instrument. Unit generators are also multiply used; only one copy of each type of generator is in the memory; memory is thus conserved.

4. A free-field format for score cards is used. Successive fields are separated by one or more blanks or by commas. Mnemonics are used to denote operation codes and unit-generator types. This form of score is easier both to write and to read than the Music IV fixed-field score.

The score is interpreted by a completely separate subroutine READ1 and the output is entirely in numerical form. Therefore, it is possible to change the form of the score simply by replacing the READ1 routine. Moreover, since all subsequent parts of the program are strictly numerical, a maximum of machine independence is achieved in the FØRTRAN programs.

Overview of Music V

A block diagram of the over-all operation of the programs is shown in Fig. 48. The main programs, the principal subroutines, the flow of control, and the flow of data are indicated. The few basic machine-language programs are especially marked.

Pass I causes the score to be read by the READ1 subroutine. The score may be thought of as a sequence of data cards prepared by the user, although the actual medium could also be a computer-connected typewriter, a graphic computer, or a data file.

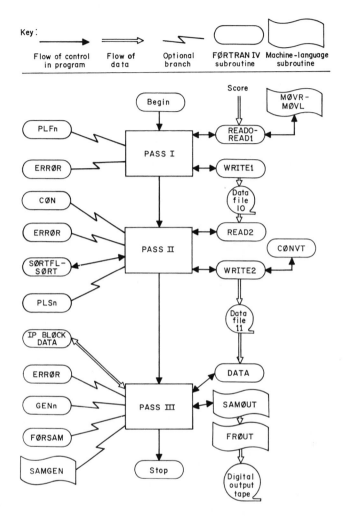

Fig. 48. Block diagram of Music V operation.

Cards are processed by Pass I in the order in which they occur in the score. Data are grouped into data statements which are terminated by a semicolon; a data statement need not correspond to a single card. The first field of the data statement specifies an operation code, and the second field specifies an action time when the operation is to be done. This time is measured from the beginning of each section of the music. The other fields may vary depending on the particular operation code.

The total number of fields may vary; no more than necessary need be used.

The principal operations are to

(1) Cause a note to be played
(2) Define an instrument
(3) Store data in Pass I, II, or III memory
(4) Call a subroutine in Pass I or II
(5) Generate and store a function in Pass III
(6) Terminate a section or a composition.

Pass I calls several subroutines. The function of the READ and ERRØR subroutines are obvious. The PLF subroutines are note-processing and generating routines which the composer has the option to provide if he wishes to make use of this possibility. MØVR and MØVL are two short machine-language routines that move a character to the right and left end, respectively, of the computer word. These are two of the few essential machine-language routines that must be provided.

Data statements are sent to Pass II via a data file recorded on disk or tape. Each statement is still labeled with an action time in the second field. The principal function of Pass II is to sort the data statements into ascending order of action times. (In Pass I, action times need not be ordered; in Pass III a strictly ascending order is required.) The sorting is carried out by two subroutines, SØRTFL and SØRT. These are provided as FØRTRAN IV routines; however, the sorting process can be substantially speeded by writing or obtaining machine language versions. Sorting programs are quite generally available.

After sorting the data statements for time, Pass II (optionally) applies a metronome function to distort the time scale. Subroutine CØN is used to read the metronome markings which are stored in the Pass II memory. Gradual accelerandos and ritardandos are possible, as well as sudden changes in tempo.

User-provided subroutines, called PLS subroutines, may be optionally supplied and applied to the data records after time sorting.

Just before each data statement is sent to Pass III, a CØNVT subroutine operates on all its fields. CØNVT must be supplied by the user; it replaces all the CVT routines in Music IV. For example, it is often given the job of converting frequency notation from some humanly simple scale like 12 tones—1...12—to the proper input numbers for oscillator frequency control. Inputs for attack and decay generators are conveniently computed here. Frequently, CØNVT adds parameters to the data statement.

The actual acoustic samples are computed in Pass III. The unit generators are encoded in SAMGEN (in basic machine language) and FØRSAM (in FØRTRAN IV). The Pass III program organizes these unit generators into instruments and plays the instruments as specified by the score. In addition, the GEN routines may be called upon to compute functions that are stored in the Pass III memory and are referred to by unit generators (e.g., ØSC).

Data statements which are the input of Pass III have action times written in their second field; these action times are now monotonically ordered; they determine the times at which all processing and generating in Pass III are performed.

Almost all information in Pass III is stored in one large array called I. It contains instrument definitions, parameters of notes currently being played, stored functions (from GEN routines), input–output blocks for unit generators, and certain other data. The size of I can be adjusted to a particular machine by an appropriate dimension statement.

Various other essential parameters—such as the length of a stored function, the number of stored functions, the length and number of input–output blocks, the maximum number of simultaneously sounding voices—will change with different computers and compositions. These parameters have been assembled into the IP array, which is compiled by a BLØCK DATA subprogram. Hence the parameters can be easily changed.

The usual unit generators and GEN functions use fixed-point arithmetic and store their results in the I array. (It would not be difficult to use floating-point routines instead, or to use both.) However, the routines do not produce FØRTRAN integers. Instead, FØRTRAN fixed-point numbers are multiplied by 2^n, which in effect puts their decimal points n places from the right end of the memory words. Values of 2^n for unit generators and for GEN functions are also compiled into the IP array. These values can be changed to accommodate different lengths of memory word.

Output samples are written on a digital output tape by a combination of SAMØUT and FRØUT subroutines. These are inherently machine-language operations, and there is no way to avoid so writing them. However, they can be brief and demand little programming time.

Chapter 3, which presents the Music V manual, is organized in the same manner as the program; it starts with a discussion of Pass I and its subroutines and then proceeds to the other passes. The actual FØRTRAN programs are, of course, the ultimate and best description of Music V; they should be read along with the manual.

2. Description of Pass I

The purpose of Pass I is to read the input data (score) and translate it into a form acceptable to the subsequent passes. The operation is diagrammed in Fig. 49.

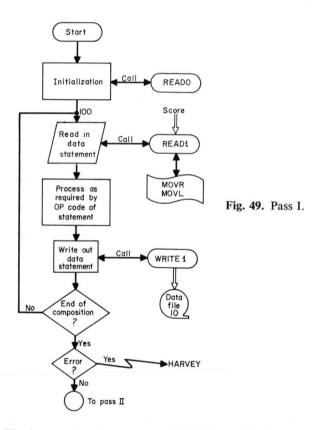

Fig. 49. Pass I.

The interpretive input routine READ1 (and READ0, which is used to read the first record) is written in FØRTRAN IV. It is designed for a computer with a word length of 36 bits. It requires two user-supplied subroutines (MØVL, MØVR) to be written in machine language for purposes of character shifting. Minor modifications to READ0 and

READ1 are necessary for computers of different word length and for different modes of input (see Section 7 for details).

The input data comprise a series of data statements punched in free format in columns 1 through 72 of cards. A data statement need not correspond to a single card.

A data statement begins with an operation code and is terminated by a semicolon. Other fields of information in the statement are separated by blanks (any number) or commas. Null fields, i.e., those denoted by successive commas, are assumed to have the value 0. With the exception of statements used in instrument definitions (see Section 4), the fields of a data statement are referred to as P fields since they load sequentially into the P array located in CØMMØN storage in Pass I.[2] The operation code, written as a three-letter mnemonic (see Section 3) is converted to a numerical equivalent and goes into P(1); the second field, containing an action time that specifies when the operation corresponding to the code is to be performed, goes into P(2). The other fields are interpreted according to the specifications of the various operation codes. If a field other than the OP code is written as an asterisk (*), the value stored in the corresponding position of the P array will be the value previously stored there. This feature can be employed to advantage when parameters remain constant over a sequence of data statements.

The input data are terminated with the data statement having the operation code of TER. Failure to provide this statement will result in an error comment.

The input program makes certain checks on the data statements and when errors are detected the value of IP(2), located in CØMMØN storage, is set to 1. Since this location is initially 0, Pass I can verify at its conclusion whether or not errors have been detected and, if so, the run is terminated without proceeding to Pass II. Termination is accomplished by calling a nonexistent subroutine named HARVEY.

As the data cards are read, they are printed, and any error comments are printed out after the offending statement. Data statements beginning with operation code CØM result only in printing and are not processed further. Such statements may be used to annotate the input data with comments.

In addition to establishing the appropriate values in the P fields, READ1 counts the number of P fields in the data statement and sets IP(1) (in CØMMØN storage) to this count. Pass I is then able to process the data statement as is required by the operation code and to write

[2] CØMMØN storage in Pass I is arranged according to the statement, CØMMØN IP(10), P(100), D(2000)

out the translated statement as N, (P(I), I = 1, N), where N = IP(1), to be read by Pass II.

Pass I contains a data array D(2000) which may be used for general storage and may in particular contain data for the PLF subroutines. SV1 and SIA data statements load the D array. (SV1 0 10 100; would set D(10) = 100.) The following D variables have special significance.

D(4) = Sampling rate

D(8) = Stereo-mono flag

D(8) = 1   for stereo

D(8) = 0   for mono

3. Operation Codes and Corresponding Data Statements

The operation codes are listed in the following table.

Numerical Value	Mnemonic	Purpose
1	NØT	Play note
2	INS	Define instrument
3	GEN	Generate function
4	SV3	Set variable in Pass III
5	SEC	End section
6	TER	Terminate piece
7	SV1	Set variable in Pass I
8	SV2	Set variable in Pass II
9	PLF	Execute subroutine in Pass I
10	PLS	Execute subroutine in Pass II
11	SI3	Set integer in Pass III
12	SIA	Set integer in all passes
13[a]	CØM	Print comment

[a] This code number is used only by READ1. A data statement beginning with CØM is printed but is not processed further.

Remarks

1. Only the first three characters of the operation code mnemonic are scanned; thus a user may write NØTE, INSTRUMENT, GEN-ERATE, SECTIØN, TERMINATE, or CØMMENT in place of the three-letter codes if he prefers.

2. Integer-valued P fields may be written with or without decimal points.

3. Null fields, those denoted by successive commas, are assumed to be 0.

4. Fields specified as * are assumed to have the value previously stored there. This feature provides continuation over a sequence of data statements.

Description of Data Statements

Each statement begins with the mnemonic operation code (at least three letters). The second field must contain the time at which the operation is to be performed. Therefore the descriptions that follow the specifications will begin with the third field. All statements are terminated by a semicolon.

1. NØT—Play note
   - P(3) Number of instrument on which note is to be played
   - P(4) Duration of note (in beats)
   - P(5)... As desired by instrument referred to in P(3)
2. INS—Define instrument
   - P(3) Number of instrument being defined
3. GEN—Generate a function
   - P(3) Number of generating subroutine (see Section 25)
   - P(4) Number of function to be generated
   - P(5)... As required by generating subroutine
4. SV3—Set variable(s) in Pass III, starting with variable N
   - P(3) Number of first variable to set = N
   - P(4) Value of variable N
   - P(5) Value of variable N + 1
   - P(6) ... (Number of variables to be set is automatically determined by the word count.)
5. SEC—End section and reset time scale to zero
6. TER—Terminate piece at specified time relative to last section
7. SV1—Set variable(s) in Pass I, starting with variable N
   - P(3) Number of first variable to set = N
   - P(4) Value of variable N
   - P(5) Value of variable N + 1
   - P(6) ... (Number of variables to be set is determined by the word count.)
8. SV2—Set variable in Pass II
   - Fields are as in SV1
9. PLF—Execute subroutine in Pass I
   - P(3) Number of subroutine: 1, 2, 3, 4, or 5
   - P(4)... As required by subroutine referred to in P(3)

10. PLS—Execute subroutine in Pass II
Fields are as in PLF

11. SI3—Set integer(s) in Pass III, starting with integer N
P(3) Number of first integer to be set = N
P(4) Value of integer N
P(5) Value of integer N + 1
P(6) ... (Number of integers to be set is determined by the word count.)

12. SIA—Set integer(s) in all passes
P(3) Number of first integer to be set = N
P(4) Value of integer N
P(5) Value of integer N + 1
P(6) ... (Number of integers to be set is determined by the word count.)

4. Definition of Instruments

An instrument definition begins with the data statement "INS t n;" where t specifies the time at which instrument n is to be defined. Subsequent data statements indicate the unit generators used in the instrument and their associated parameters. The data statement "END;" terminates the definition.

The unit generators that are recognized by name (i.e., three-letter mnemonic) by READ1 follow.

Name	Parameters	Type Number	Purpose
ØUT	I1, Ø ;	1	Monophonic output
ØSC	I1, I2, Ø, F, S ;	2	Oscillator
AD2	I1, I2, Ø ;	3	Two-input adder
RAN	I1, I2, Ø, S, T1, T2 ;	4	Random function generator
ENV	I1, F, Ø, A, SS, D, S ;	5	Envelope generator
STR	I1, I2, Ø ;	6	Stereophonic output
AD3	I1, I2, I3, Ø ;	7	Three-input adder
AD4	I1, I2, I3, I4, Ø ;	8	Four-input adder
MLT	I1, I2, Ø ;	9	Multiplier
FLT	I1, I2, I3, Ø ;	10	Filter
RAH	I1, I2, Ø, S, T ;	11	Random and hold function generator
SET	I1 ;	102	Set new function

See Section 5 for a more complete description of the unit generators.

Data statements that specify unit generators may begin with the three-letter mnemonic name or with the type number. READ1 recognizes the 12 types listed in the table above by name,[3] and makes a check on the proper number of parameters. If, for example, four or six parameters are listed for ØSC, which requires five parameters, an error condition will result, causing the job to terminate at the conclusion of Pass I after all input cards have been scanned. Since unit generators may be labeled by type number as well as name, it is possible to add units to the subroutines FØRSAM (coded in FØRTRAN IV) or SAMGEN (coded in basic machine language) used in Pass III without the need for modifying READ1. Data statements referring to these new units by type number will be accepted by READ1, but no check will be made for proper number of parameters.

The notation for these parameters used on the data statement is as follows:

Pn refers to nth P field on note card
Vn refers to nth location in variable storage of Pass III
Fn refers to nth stored function
Bn refers to nth I-Ø block used by units

For example, instrument No. 3 would be defined at t = 10 by the following data statements:

INS 10 3 ;
ØSC P5 P6 B2 F1 P30 ;
AD2 P7 V1 B3 ;
ØSC B2 B3 B2 F2 P29 ;
ØUT B2 B1;
END ;

READ1 translates each mnemonic data statement into an all-numerical data statement as follows:

(1) In all data statements, P1 contains 2, the numerical equivalent of INS, and P2 contains the action time (10 in the example).
(2) P3 contains the instrument number (3) in the first data statement.
(3) In the second through the last data statements, P3–Pn contains the numerical equivalent of the mnemonic data statement fields $P1 \ldots P_{last}$, respectively. The name equivalents for the unit generators are their type numbers listed above. The equivalents of the P's, V's, etc., are as follows:

[3] The "named" generators change frequently. The table describes the state of affairs in April 1968 at Bell Laboratories.

$$Pm \rightarrow m \qquad\qquad 1 \le m \le 100$$
$$Vn \rightarrow 100 + n$$
$$Fp \rightarrow -(100 + p)$$
$$Bq \rightarrow -q \qquad\qquad 1 \le q \le 100$$

The equivalents are unique because only 100 P's and 100 B's are allowed. P's are represented by positive numbers from 1 to 100, V's by positive numbers greater than 100, B's by negative numbers from -1 to -100, and F's by negative numbers from -101 to $-\infty$.

(4) The last mnemonic data statement, END, has only two fields, P1 = 2 and P2 = action time. It is recognized in Pass III by its word count of 2; this terminates the instrument definition.

The example is translated into the following numerical data statements:

```
2 10 3 ;
2 10 2 5 6 −2 −101 30 ;
2 10 3 7 101 −3 ;
2 10 2 −2 −3 −2 −102 29 ;
2 10 1 −2 −1 ;
2 10 ;
```

All passes of the program operate exclusively on the numerical statements; all mnemonics are translated by READ1.

5. Unit Generators

ØUT: Output Unit (Numerical equivalent = 1)
Diagram:

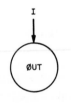

Data statement: ØUT, I, Ø ;
Operation: This unit generator adds the specified input into the specified output block thus combining it with any other instrument that concurrently uses the output block. $Ø_i = Ø_i + I_i$ where i denotes the ith sample.

Example: One of the simplest
instruments is defined as
INS, 0, 1 ;
ØSC, P5, P6, B2, F1, P20 ;
ØUT, B2, B1 ;
END ;

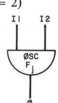

B1 is often used as the output block. The location of the output block must be compiled into IP(10) (see Section 17).

ØSC: Oscillator (Numerical equivalent = 2)
Diagram:

Data statement: ØSC, I1, I2, Ø, Fj, S ;
Operation: The oscillator generates functions and oscillations according to

$$\varnothing_i = I1_i \cdot F_j([S_i] \text{ mod function length in samples})$$

and

$$S_{i+1} = S_i + I2_i$$
$$S_0 = \text{initial value of sum}$$

where $\varnothing_i$ is output, $I1_i$ is amplitude, F_j is a (stored) function, S_i is the sum, $I2_i$ (increment) determines the frequency of oscillation, and i indexes the samples.

The frequency of the oscillation is

$$\text{Frequency} = \frac{\text{sampling rate} \times I2}{\text{function length in samples}}$$

The length of the function in samples is equal to IP(6) − 1. n (which = IP(6)) samples of each function are stored. The first and nth samples represent the same point on the function and must have the same value. Hence the function is periodic with period $n - 1$ sample times. One note parameter P_n must be reserved for the sum. The value of this parameter on the data statement determines the initial value of the sum S_0. Usually n is selected to be one of the last locations in note parameter storage; if P_n is not written on the note card (cf. Section 4) P_n is automatically set to zero at the beginning of each note.

Example: The example for the output box is also appropriate for the oscillator. F1 determines the wave shape. P5 is the amplitude. P6 determines the frequency. Specifically

$$\text{Frequency} = \frac{\text{P6} \times \text{sampling rate}}{\text{function length in samples}}$$

See Chapter 2, section on ØSC Generator, and Chapter 3, Section 6, for more details about ØSC.

AD2, AD3, AD4: Two-, Three-, and Four-Input Adders (Numerical equivalent = 3; AD3 = 7; AD4 = 8)
Diagram:

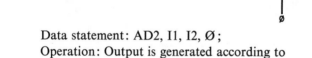

Data statement: AD2, I1, I2, Ø;
Operation: Output is generated according to

$$\emptyset_i = \text{I1}_i + \text{I2}_i$$

The other adding units (AD3 and AD4) work in a manner analogous to AD2.

Example: None.

RAN: Random Function Generator (Numerical equivalent = 4)
Diagram:

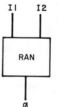

Data statement: RAN, I1, I2, Ø, S, T1, T2;

Operation: Output is generated according to

$$\emptyset_i = I1_i * R_i(I2_i)$$

RAN generates a low-pass random function whose peak amplitude is $I1_i$ and whose cutoff frequency is controlled by $I2_i$ and is approximately

$$B \approx \frac{\text{sampling rate}}{2} \cdot \frac{I2_i}{512}$$

More specifically, R_i is a function, varying from -1 to $+1$, obtained by sampling the line segments that connect independent random numbers, N_i. There are $512/I2$ samples between each pair of independent random numbers (see Fig. 50). The N_i's are uniformly distributed from -1 to $+1$.

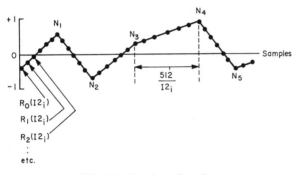

Fig. 50. Random function.

S, T1, and T2 are temporary storage locations which are normally kept in note-parameter locations. S holds a sum equivalent to the ØSC sum. T1 holds N_{i-1} and T2 holds $N_i - N_{i-1}$ where N_{i-1} and N_i are the last two independent random numbers.

Example: A typical instrument to produce a band-pass noise:

INS, 0, 1;
RAN, P5, P6, B2, P30, P28, P27;
ØSC, B2, P7, B2, F1, P29;
ØUT, B2, B1;
END;

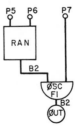

Function F1 is assumed to be a sine wave. By means of the modulation inherent in the multiplication of the left oscillator input, B2 will contain samples of a band-pass noise whose center frequency is

$$\frac{P7 \times \text{sampling rate}}{\text{function length}}$$

and whose bandwidth is

$$\frac{P6 \times \text{sampling rate}}{512}$$

The peak amplitude is P5.

ENV: Envelope Generator (Numerical equivalent = 5)
Diagram:

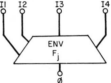

Data statement: ENV, I1, F_j, $\emptyset$, I2, I3, I4, S ;
Operation: This unit scans a function F_j at a variable rate to produce an attack, steady-state, and decay amplitude envelope on a note.

$$\emptyset_i = I1_i * F_j \quad \text{(scanned according to I2, I3, and I4)}$$

The first quarter of F_j gives the attack shape, the second quarter of F_j gives the steady state, the third quarter of F_j gives the decay shape, the fourth quarter is unused and should be zero.

Specifically, the sections of F_j and the scanning rates are shown in Fig. 51.

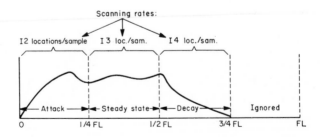

Fig. 51. Envelope function. FL = function length in samples.

In a typical use

$$I2 = \frac{\text{function length in samples}}{4 \cdot \text{attack time} \cdot \text{sampling rate}}$$

$$I3 = \frac{\text{function length in samples}}{4 \cdot \text{steady-state time} \cdot \text{sampling rate}}$$

$$I4 = \frac{\text{function length in samples}}{4 \cdot \text{decay time} \cdot \text{sampling rate}}$$

S is a temporary storage location (note parameter) to store a sum similar to the sum in ØSC.

Example: The principal use is
to generate envelopes
for notes.
INS, 0, 1 ;
ENV, P5, F1, B2, P6, P7, P8, P20 ;
ØSC, B2, P9, B2, F2, P19 ;
ØUT, B2, B1 ;
END ;

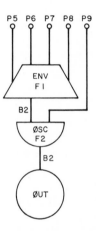

P6, P7, and P8 determine attack, steady state, and decay times, respectively. P5 determines the maximum amplitude. P9 determines the frequency. F1 determines the envelope and F2 the oscillator waveshape. Typically P6, P7, and P8 are computed by an elaborate CØNVT function (see Chapter 2, section on Additional Unit Generators, ENV).

STR: Stereophonic Output Box (Numerical equivalent = 6)
Diagram:

Data statement: STR, I1, I2, Ø ;

Operation: This unit puts alternate samples from I1 and I2 into Ø

$$\emptyset_{2i} = I1_i$$
$$\emptyset_{2i+1} = I2_i$$

This arrangement is suitable for a stereophonic output conversion.

The stereophonic output requires an output block length equal to *two* input–output block lengths. Typically B1 and B2 are set aside for output storage.

Example: Two instruments are defined
which are identical except
that one uses the left
channel and the other the
right.
INS, 0, 1 ;
ØSC, P5, P6, B3, F1, P20 ;
STR, B3, V1, B1 ;
END ;
INS, 0, 2 ;
ØSC, P5, P6, B3, F1, P20 ;
STR, V1, B3, B1 ;
END ;

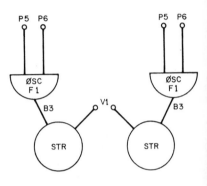

V1 is assumed to be zero. Note that blocks B1 and B2 have been reserved for output.

In another example, a single instrument produces sound in both right and left channels.

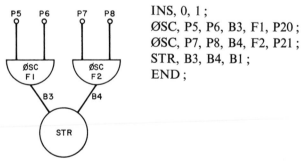

INS, 0, 1 ;
ØSC, P5, P6, B3, F1, P20 ;
ØSC, P7, P8, B4, F2, P21 ;
STR, B3, B4, B1 ;
END ;

RAH: Random and Hold Function Generator (Numerical equivalent = 11)
Diagram:

Data statement: RAH, I1, I2, Ø, S, T;
Operation: Output is generated according to

$$\emptyset_i = I1_i \times R_n(I2_i)$$

where $R_n(I2_i)$ is a succession of independent random numbers which change every $512/I2$ samples. Thus this generator holds each random number for $512/I2$ samples. $R_n(I2_i)$ is uniformly distributed from -1 to $+1$.

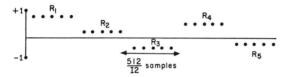

S and T are temporary storage locations which are normally kept in note parameter locations. S holds a sum equivalent to the ØSC sum· T holds the current R_i.

Example: A typical instrument
to produce a succession
of random pitches:
INS, 0, 1;
RAH, P7, P8, B2, P20, P19;
AD2, P6, B2, B2;
ØSC, P5, B2, B2, F1, P18;
ØUT, B2, B1;
END;

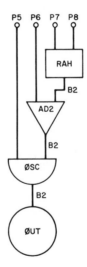

Function F1 can be any desired waveform. P7 should be at most equal to P6. The pitch frequency will assume a succession of random values between the frequencies

$$\frac{(P6 - P7) \times \text{sampling rate}}{\text{function length}}$$

and

$$\frac{(P6 + P7) \times \text{sampling rate}}{\text{function length}}$$

A new value of the pitch frequency is generated every 512/P8 samples.

SET: Set New Function Number in Unit Generator (Numerical equivalent = 102)
Diagram:

Data statement: SET, I1 ;
Operation: SET enables changing the function number in an ØSC or ENV unit generator by specifying the new function number as a note parameter.

In the instrument definition, SET must be just ahead of the unit generator on which it is to act; the input specifies in which P field of the note card the new function number is to appear. If this P field is given a negative or zero value, no change is effected; if it is given a positive integer value, this value is the new function number.

Example: INS, 0, 1 ;
         SET, P7 ;
         ØSC, P5, P6, B2, F1, P20 ;
         ØUT, B2, B1 ;
         END ;

With this instrument definition, all three of the following note cards

    NØT, 0, 1, 1, 1000, 50, 0 ;
    NØT, 1, 1, 1, 1000, 50, 1 ;
    NØT, 2, 1, 1, 1000, 50, −2 ;

will leave function #1 in ØSC, whereas the note card

    NØT, 3, 1, 1, 1000, 50, 2 ;

replaces function #1 by function #2 in ØSC.

6. Special Discussion of ØSC Unit Generator [4]

Probably the most basic and important unit generator used by Music V is the oscillator. Since the oscillator utilizes most of the basic

[4] This discussion of ØSC was provided by S. C. Johnson.

principles of Music V, a detailed description of its operation should prove useful in the design and implementation of additional unit generators.

The oscillator is a unit generator, meaning that it is a "device" that is useful in building "instruments." This device is simulated by a general computational *algorithm* which can produce any periodic function at any frequency or amplitude. This algorithm should be quite efficient, since it must compute 10,000–20,000 numbers for each second of sound.

Efficiency and generality are gained through the use of *stored functions*. The values of a stored function need be computed only once (by a GEN subroutine in Music V) and then may be referred to by any unit generator. By making the functions interchangeable among unit generators, we need keep only one copy of any function used and one copy of any unit generator in the computer memory.

The mathematical algorithm for simulating an oscillator is described by the equation

$$\emptyset_i = A_i \cdot F(S_i \bmod FL)$$

and

$$S_{i+1} = S_i + I_i$$

where

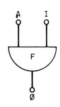

$\emptyset_i$ = the ith output sample
A_i = the ith amplitude input
I_i = the ith increment input (controls frequency)
F = a stored function (controls waveshape)
S_i = the ith sum of increments
FL = the length of the stored function (in samples)

Assume for a moment that the stored function is a representation of a sine wave occupying 101 computer locations, $F(0), F(2), \ldots, F(100)$.

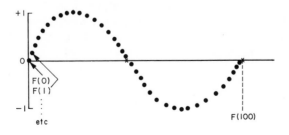

The value of F(0) is sin (0/100 * 2π), F(1) is sin (1/100 * 2π), F(2) is sin (2/100 * 2π), etc. Since $0 \leq |\sin x| \leq 1.0$, we may multiply the values of the function by any amplitude A to produce output samples in the desired range, $0 \leq |\emptyset_i| \leq A$.

How does the oscillator reproduce this sine wave at any frequency? Assume that we have fixed the sampling rate at 10,000 samples per second. This means that the digital-to-analog converter will convert 10,000 samples into sound every second, and each sample number we output represents 1/10,000 second of sound. If we multiply the stored function shown above by an appropriate amplitude and output it directly, then each period of the wave will contain 100 samples, and it will be heard 10,000/100 or 100 times per second. This corresponds to a frequency of 100 Hz. Since the sampling rate is fixed, to double the frequency of the sound we must halve the number of samples per period of the wave. We do this simply by referring to *every other* value of the stored function.

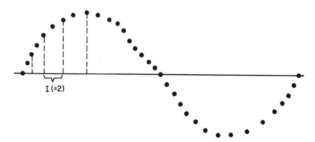

Thus the output samples will be given by the relations

$$\emptyset(1) = F(0) * A \quad (s = 0)$$
$$\emptyset(2) = F(2) * A \quad (s = 2)$$
$$\emptyset(3) = F(4) * A \quad (s = 4)$$
$$\vdots$$

etc.

The output wave then has 50 samples per period and is heard at 10,000/50 or 200 Hz. To obtain the output $\emptyset_i$ in this case, the independent variable in the function F(s) is incremented by 2 each time the function is referred to. If the increment used was 4, we would output 100/4 = 25 samples per period, or a sine wave of 10,000/25 or 400 Hz. In general then

$$\text{Frequency in hertz} = \frac{\text{sampling rate}}{\text{samples per period}}$$

and

$$\text{Samples per period} = \frac{\text{function length}}{\text{increment}}$$

therefore,

$$\text{Frequency in hertz} = \frac{\text{sampling rate} * \text{increment}}{\text{function length}}$$

and

$$\text{Increment (in samples)} = \frac{\text{function length} * \text{frequency in hertz}}{\text{sampling rate}}$$

Modulus arithmetic is used in conjunction with the cumulative sum of increments S_i in order to achieve periodicity in the references to the stored function.

A final point concerns the sum of increments. Assuming a function length and sampling rate as above, the increment necessary to produce a 150-Hz tone I is $(100 * 150)/10,000$ or 1.5. Obviously any continuous function will have a value at $S = 1.5$, but we cannot directly talk about the 1.5th computer location of stored function F. Three approaches to this problem have been used: truncation, rounding, and interpolation. The fastest method is truncation, where the greatest integer $[S]$ contained in the sum of increments is used as the S value. This is easily accomplished with fixed-point computer arithmetic, but may lead to some distortion of the output (see the table below). In the rounding method, we round the sum of increments to the *nearest* integer and use this as the S value. Although this takes a little more computation, it leads to better results.

In the interpolation method, the sum of increments is truncated to obtain a function value as in the truncation method. This function value is then corrected by linear interpolation: if y is the function value at $F([S])$, y′ is the function value at $F([S] + 1)$, and h is the amount by which the sum of increments exceeds $[S]$ ($= S - [S]$, or the *fractional part*), then the corrected value of the function is $y + (y' - y)h$. This method takes the most computer time but in practice produces the greatest accuracy. It can also effect a saving of memory space in the computer, since, as is shown in the table below, treating a stored function of 512 locations with truncation produces a greater distortion of the output than using interpolation on a function only 32 locations long.

The table shows the results of computing 500 values of sine x, using various methods and stored function lengths. The table entries are the percentage rms error.

Function Length	Truncation	Rounding	Interpolation
32	7.9	4.0	0.3
64	3.8	1.9	0.06
128	1.7	1.1	0.02
256	0.9	0.5	0.004
512	0.5	0.2	0.001
1024	0.24	0.12	0.0002

In general, rounding is about twice as accurate as truncation, and doubling the length of the stored function doubles the accuracy for both the truncation and rounding. Doubling the function length quadruples the accuracy for the interpolation method, however. Which method is used will depend on the availability of computer time versus memory space in a particular installation of Music V.

The distortion level of the oscillator depends on the function length and the particular numeral process used. It also depends on the particular increment used: distortion occurs only when the increment is not an integer. Finally, it depends on the waveshape used: the distortion level will increase when the slope of the stored function is steep at the point considered.

How much this distortion alters the quality of the sound is hard to predict; a function with steep slope should be expected to be more distorted than a sine wave, and yet in many cases the distortion will be more *audible* with sine waves than with complex waveforms. For instance, the synthesis of a frequency-modulated sine wave with the following parameters:

Function length = 512 samples
Sampling rate = 10,000 Hz
Frequency deviation = 3% (of fundamental frequency)
Vibrato rate = 25% (of fundamental frequency)

produces a clearly distorted sound when truncation is used, and an acceptable sound when interpolation is used. But if the sine wave is replaced by a complex tone with harmonies decreasing at 6 dB or 12 dB per octave, there is almost no audible difference between sounds synthesized with truncation and those synthesized with interpolation.

7. Input–Output Routines for Pass I and Pass II

Input for Pass I: READ0 and READ1

The interpretative input routine for Pass I is a FØRTRAN IV sub-routine named READ1. It has an additional entry point called READ0 used for reading the first record. The program, as supplied with Music V, is designed for a 36-bit word machine and accepts input data punched in the free format in columns 1 through 72 of cards, as has been described in Section 3.

READ0 reads an initial record into the input buffer ICAR (equivalent to CARD). The characters are stored one per computer word and are shifted to the right end of the word by the MØVR subroutine. (MØVR is one of the machine-language routines necessary for Music V.)

The operation of READ1, the main program, is diagrammed in Fig. 52. After writing out a record to set Music V to stereo or mono (which will be discussed below), the program (at 10)[5] scans to the end of the first data statement marked by ";". If necessary, more input records are read.

The characters are organized (at 21) into fields with exactly one blank character separating successive fields. The organized data are stored in IBCD and are printed out. The first field is compared with all possible mnemonics that may be written in it. If a match is found, the numerical equivalent of the mnemonic is found and one of a number of branches (at 29) is taken depending on the value of the first field.

If no match is found for the first field (at 40), it is taken to be a number if the data statement is inside an instrument definition. Otherwise, an error comment is made and the statement is rejected.

The remaining fields on the data statement are converted to numerical form by one of several sections of the program (218, 201–210, 100, 300–1200, 200, 217, 220, and 30) depending on what the first field is and whether the data statement is part of an instrument definition.

All score records have a mnemonic operation code as the first field and an action time as a second field *except* the second through the last cards in an instrument definition. In an instrument definition, such as the one given below

> INS, Action time, Inst No ;
> ØSC, P5, P6, B2, F1, P20 ;
> ØUT, B2, B1 ;
> END :

---

[5] The numbers cited in the descriptions of programs refer to statement numbers in the FØRTRAN program. These numbers are also shown in the block diagrams.

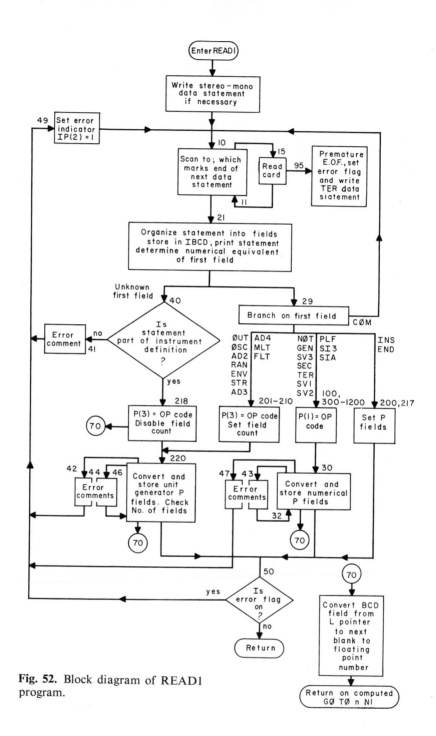

Fig. 52. Block diagram of READ1 program.

the operation code and action time appear only on the first data record. READ1 takes the operation code ($= 2$) and the action time from the first data record and stores these in P(1) and P(2) in all subsequent records connected with instrument definition. The value of P(3) is the type number of the unit, and the remaining fields are interpreted and converted to floating point and stored starting in P(4). Word (i.e., field) count for the statement is established in IP(1).

The conversion from BCD to floating point is done by a subroutine (at 70) which finds the position of the decimal point in the field of characters (or supplies it at the end if missing) and then multiplies the characters, which are expressed as integers, by the appropriate power of 10 and sums over all characters in the field.

Any errors that are detected cause an error comment to be printed below the printout of the data statement in which the error occurred. In cases other than that of an incorrect operation code, the entire statement is scanned so that all errors will be detected. Incorrect operation codes, however, prevent proper interpretation of the remaining fields in the data statement. When errors occur, a flag is set in CØMMØN storage (namely IP(2) is set to 1) so that Pass I may terminate the job at its conclusion. Furthermore, when errors are detected, the data statement is not returned to Pass I but control returns to the entry point of READ1 to obtain the next data statement.

It will be noted that the input array for the card data is named CARD which is (FØRTRAN) equivalent to ICAR. Also, IBCD is equivalent to BCD. This equivalence is necessary because the characters when read in with format A1 require a floating-point designation. However, for purposes of comparison, the data must be regarded as in integer form. Hence, the characters must be right adjusted (moved to the right and of the computer word). Similarly, when the organized data statement is to be printed out, it must be put back into left-adjusted form so that it may be printed out in A1 format. Consequently, this routine uses two subroutines, which must be written in machine language and, therefore, supplied by the user. READ1 (and READ0) makes the following calls:

CALL MØVR (CARD, NC)
CALL MØVL (CARD, NC)

The characters stored in NC consecutive locations of CARD are right (left) adjusted and replaced in the same locations. Calls to MØVR are found after the two "read" statements, and the "print" statement is preceded by a call to MØVL and followed by a call to MØVR.

READ1 inspects the output unit generators (ØUT or STR) in the instruments, and if a change from monophonic to stereophonic operation or vice versa is made, it writes out an appropriate stereo or mono control record at the end of the instrument definition. The record is

$$\text{SIA TA 8} \begin{pmatrix} 0\,(= \text{mono}) \\ 1\,(= \text{stereo}) \end{pmatrix};$$

The action time TA is the same as the action time for the instrument definition. Inspection is done by the first statement in READ1. END equals 1 at the end of an instrument definition and equals 0 otherwise. SNA8 equals 1 if the mono-stereo mode is changed and equals 0 otherwise. STER = 0 if the last out box is ØUT, and STER = 1 if the box is STR. Music V is assumed initially to be in the monaural mode.

If the program is to be run on a machine of different word length, the FØRTRAN DATA statements for arrays IBC, IVT, and LØP must be changed. These contain right-adjusted BCD characters for the break characters used in delimiting the input, the parameter types P, V, F, and B used in specifying unit generators, and the characters used in the three-letter mnemonic names for operation codes. In a 36-bit machine such data are entered as 6H00000X, in a 24-bit machine as 4H000X. If the input data are to be read in from any medium other than cards, the two "READ" statements at 15 and under READ0 need to be changed as required. The number of characters obtained by executing a "READ" command is a variable NC, established in this version of the program as 72. The arrays that hold these data have been dimensioned to accept a maximum value of NC equal to 128.

The break characters delimiting the fields of input data are the blank, comma, and semicolon; NBC, the number of break characters, is equal to 3. (If typewriter input is to be substituted, an additional break character may be needed equal to the carriage return.)

The most frequent change in READ1 is the addition of other OP codes or unit-generator names. The following steps will accomplish this change:

(1) Add the three-character mnemonic to the end of the LØP array. (The size of the LØP array may or may not need to be increased, the word count on the LØP DATA statement must be increased.)
(2) Increase NØPS by 1.
(3) Put another branch at the end of the GØ TØ at 29.

(4) Write appropriate code for the branch. The code for branches 201–210 or 300–1200 will usually serve as a model.

A few of the variables in the program are

NUMU   Normally equals 0. It is set to 1 to disable checking the number of fields in a unit generator.

NPW   The number of fields expected in a unit generator, not counting the name. For example, AD3 P1 P2 P3 B1; would have NPW = 4.

L   Scanning index for the IBCD array. It normally points to the character just ahead of the next field to be processed. L is changed by many parts of the program, including the BCD to floating-point converter.

I   Scanning index for the ICAR array.

J   Scanning index to store characters in the IBCD array.

Output for Pass I: WRITE1

The number of fields in a data statement is established by READ1 and stored in IP(1) located in CØMMØN. The fields of the data statement have been interpreted and the P array appropriately filled by READ1. Thus after Pass I has properly processed the data statement, it may call WRITE1 to write the data statement on tape or disc so as to be available to Pass II. The call from Pass I is as follows:

CALL WRITE1 (10)

WRITE1 sets N = IP(1) and writes the list N, (P(I), I = 1, N) onto data file 10 in binary format.

Input for Pass II: READ2

Pass II calls upon subroutine READ2 with the call CALL READ2 (10) to read N, (P(I), I = 1, N) from data file 10 and establish IP(1) = N.

Debug READ0 and READ1

For testing purposes, an all-FØRTRAN score-reading program is provided to replace READ0 and READ1. The program reads an all-numerical score. Each data statement has the following information:

N P(1) P(2) ... P(N)

where N is the word count and the subsequent fields destined for the first N locations of the P array.

The calling sequences are the same as those of READ0 and READ1, namely

CALL READ0

and

CALL READ1

Debug READ0 does nothing.

Debug READ1 reads one statement into the P array according to the FØRTRAN statement

READ1, K, (P(J), J = 1, K)

where the format statement 1 is

1 FØRMAT(I6, 11F6.0/(12F6.0))

Thus twelve numbers are read from the first 72 columns of each card.

8. PLF Subroutines

A data statement of the type

PLF 0 n D4 D5 ... Dm ;

will cause the following call to take place during Pass I at the time the data statement is read

CALL PLFn

where n is some integer between 1 and 5. PLFn is a subroutine which must be supplied by the user. These subroutines can perform any function desired by the user. Usually they will generate data statements for Pass II or manipulate Pass I memory (the D(2000) array).

The information of the data statement PLF, 0, n, D4, ..., Dm will be placed in the P(100) array in P(1) − P(m) at the time PLFn is called.

The P, D, and IP arrays are kept in common storage and hence are available to the PLFn routine. The dimension and common statements in the PLF routine and in Pass I must, of course, agree. For examples and a further discussion of PLF subroutines, see Chapter 2, section on Composing Subroutines—PLF.

9. General Error Subroutine

A general-purpose ERRØR subroutine is used by all three passes. A statement

CALL ERRØR(N)

will cause the following comment to be printed

ERRØR ØF TYPE N

where N is an integer.
The meaning of N is as follows

	N
Pass I errors	
Nonexistent OP code on data statement	10
Nonexistent PLF subroutine called	11
(i.e., in call PLF_n, $n < 1$, or $n > 5$)	
Pass II errors	
Too many notes in section, D or I array full	20
Incorrect OP code in Pass II	21
Incorrect OP code in Pass II	22
Nonexistent PLS subroutine called	23
(i.e., in call PLS_n, $n < 1$, or $n > 5$)	
Pass III errors	
Incorrect OP code in Pass III	1
Code is < 1 or > 12	
Too many voices simultaneously playing[a]	2
Too many voices simultaneously playing	3

[a] The maximum number of voices must be equal to or less than the number of note parameter blocks (see Section 16).

In addition to these error comments, the READ1 will print error comments if it detects errors in or cannot interpret any data statements. These comments are described in Section 7.

10. Description of Pass II

Pass II performs three general functions:

(1) Sorting the data records obtained from Pass I into forward chronological order according to starting times,
(2) Applying special conversions to some of the input data records by calling the user-supplied CØNVT subroutine, and
(3) Applying the metronomic time-scaling operations to starting times and durations.

After completing these functions, Pass II writes its output onto data file 11 for subsequent use by Pass III (if desired, a Pass II report is printed, see WRITE2 below). The entire operation may be diagrammed as shown in Fig. 53.

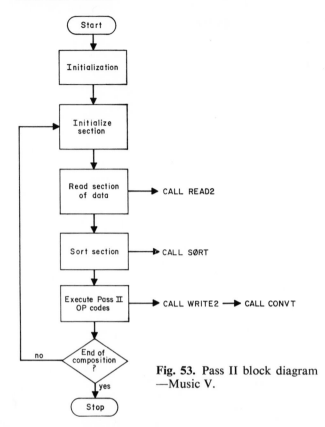

Fig. 53. Pass II block diagram —Music V.

Pass II maintains the following arrays in unlabeled common storage

CØMMØN IP(10), P(100), G(1000), I(1000), T(1000), D(10,000)

After setting certain variables (standard sampling rate, size of D and I arrays, and number of OP codes) to their initial values, Pass II calls on READ2(10). READ2 then reads information from data file 10 according to the format: (K, P(I), I = 1, K). The value of K is stored into IP(1). This call is repeated until an entire section has been read in and the data statements are accumulated in the D array. The I array is used to hold subscripts that point to the beginning of each data record in the D array. The T array is used to hold the action time of each data statement P(2). After an entire section has been read in, Pass II sorts the T array into ascending numerical order by calling SØRTFL and SØRT (SØRTFL is merely an initialization routine which informs the sort-program package that floating-point numbers are about to be sorted).

It also sorts the I array (pointers) as a passive list on T, so that after SØRT has been called this point list has been rearranged according to the starting times of the data statements.

Each data statement is then accessed from the D array according to the order specified by the I pointers (chronological order of action times). Each data statement is inspected to see:

(1) If the OP code is 8 or 12 (SV2 and SIA, respectively), then the variable list (i.e., P(4) through P(4 + n)) is stored into the G array starting at G (P(3)).

(2) If the OP code is 10 (PLS), then a call to PLS_n is generated, where n is the number stored in P(3).

(3) If the OP code is 7 or 9 (SV1 and PLF, respectively), an error message is printed (error of type 22). This error is not fatal, however, and Pass II merely ignores the offending instruction.

(4) If the OP code is 1, 2, 3, 4, 5, 6, 11, 12 (NØT, INS, GEN, SV3, SEC, TER, SI3, SIA), the subroutine WRITE2(11) is called. This subroutine applies the optional metronome time-scaling operations, prints the optional Pass II report, calls the subroutine CØNVT to modify any note parameters, and writes out a record on data file 11 for subsequent use as input to Pass III.

The record is written according to statements

K = IP(1)
WRITE(11), K, (P(J), J = 1, K)

K, which is kept in IP(1), is the word count. Data are in the P(100) array. Details of the operations done by WRITE2 are discussed in Section 11.

After a section has been processed, the next section is read. The section-reading sequence is terminated by a TER card via a flag IEND which is set to 1 when TER is encountered. IEND is checked after each section is processed.

The error comments produced by Pass II are printed by ERRØR and are discussed in Section 9.

Pass II contains a general-purpose memory, G(1000), which is primarily used by the PLS subroutines and by the CØNVT function. Blocks of locations starting at G(n) may be set with a SV2 AT n x . . . ; record. The setting occurs at the action time, AT, relative to the other data records.

Certain locations in the G array have special functions:

G(1) Flag controlling Pass II report (= 0, print report; = 1, suppress report)

G(2) Time-scaling flag (G(2) = 0 for no time scaling; G(2) = n for time scaling where metronome function starts at G(n))

G(4) Sampling rate

G(5) Starting beat of note

G(6) Duration of note in beats

G(8) Stereo-mono flag (= 0, mono; = 1, stereo)

The IP array contains certain other parameters:

IP(1) Word count for current record in P array

IP(2) Location in D array of beginning of data statement that is currently calling a PLS subroutine

IP(3) Number of data statements in the D array

11. WRITE2

Pass II calls WRITE2(11) in order to:

(1) Invoke the optional metronome operations described below

(2) Produce the optional Pass II report on the printer

(3) Call CØNVT to modify data record parameters

(4) Write (N, P(I), I = 1, N) on data file 11 for subsequent use by Pass III

In order to utilize the metronome operations available in Pass II, a nonzero value must be stored in the array location G(2). This value is the beginning subscript in the G array of a tempo function such as the one shown in Fig. 54. This is a function constructed of any number of

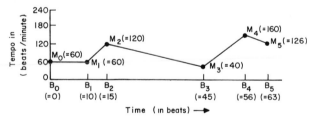

Fig. 54. Tempo function.

line segments. It is stored, beginning at G(G(2)), as an arbitrary-length list of number pairs, B_0 (= 0), M_0, B_1, M_1, B_2, M_2, ..., B_n, M_n where M_i is the standard metronome marking (in beats per minute) at beat

B_i of the composition. See Chapter 2, section on Compositional Functions, for additional discussion.

WRITE2 uses the FØRTRAN function CØN(G, I, T) (see Section 12) to calculate the value at beat T of the function which is stored at G(I). WRITE2 then converts P(2), the starting time, and P(4), the duration,[6] from beats to seconds according to the following two relationships:

$$T_i = T_{i-1} + (B_i - B_{i-1}) \cdot \left(\frac{60}{F(B_i)}\right)$$

where

T_i is current time in seconds, which replaces the value in P(2)
B_i is current beat number, the value found in P(2)
$F(B_i)$ is the value of the tempo function at beat B_i and
T_{i-1} and B_{i-1} are the time and beat of the previous data record

and

$$D_i = L_i \cdot \left(\frac{60}{F(B_i)}\right)$$

where

D_i is the duration in seconds
L_i is the duration of note in beats and
$F(B_i)$ is as above

The tempo function itself may be placed into the G array via an SV2 instruction. The function shown in Fig. 54, for example, could be placed in the G array beginning at G(30) by the data records:

SV2, 0, 2, 30 ;
SV2, 0, 30, 0, 60, 10, 60, 15, 120, 45, 40, 56, 160, 63, 126 ;

These metronome operations can be turned off at any time by setting G(2) at 0. If the metronome operations are so turned off, P(2) and P(4) are not affected by WRITE2 and are assumed to be in seconds.

The Pass II report is printed automatically by WRITE2 if G(1) = 0. The Pass II report may be suppressed by setting G(1) ≠ 0 with an SV2 instruction (e.g., SV2, 0, 1, 1 ;). It consists of each data statement printed in order of ascending action times. Each data statement is shown exactly as it is presented to Pass III (if the data statements do

---

[6] Durations are given on NØT cards only. P(4) is affected if and only if P(1) = 1 (play a note).

not exceed 10 fields, they are printed one per line; longer data statements are continued on next line). In addition, if the metronome function is in use, P(2) and P(4) will have been converted into seconds, and the original values of these parameters (in beats) are printed to the right of each print line.

WRITE2 calls CØNVT immediately before it returns. G(5) and G(6) contain the original values of P(2) and P(4) if metronomic scaling was used.

12. CØN—Function Evaluator for Line-Segment Functions

CØN evaluates functions formed from a sequence of line segments. These functions are useful for representing compositional functions such as the metronomic marking. CØN is used by the time-scaling routines in Pass II. It may also be used by PLF and PLS subroutines.

CØN can be evoked by a statement such as

$$Y = CØN(G, I, T)$$

which will set Y equal to the value at time T of the function stored at G(I).

CØN expects to find a pair list in the G array beginning at subscript I. The form of the list is $X_1, Y_1, X_2, \ldots, X_n, Y_n$, where X_i and Y_i are the abscissa and ordinate values for the breakpoints of the function. As many breakpoints as desired may be used. Breakpoints do not need to be equally spaced along the abscissa. If T falls between two breakpoints (as it usually does), CØN computes Y as a linear interpolation between the adjacent breakpoints.

As an example, the function shown in Fig. 55 would be stored starting at G(30) in Pass II by the statement

$$SV2 \ 0 \ 30 \ 0 \ 1 \ 10 \ 12 \ 20 \ 1 \ ;$$

Its value at 13 would be obtained by

$$Y = CØN(G, 30, 13) = 8.7$$

13. SØRT AND SØRTFL

SØRT and SØRTFL are two utility routines in the Bell Laboratories utility library on the GE645 computer. They are called by Pass II when it arranges the data statements in chronological order according to action times.

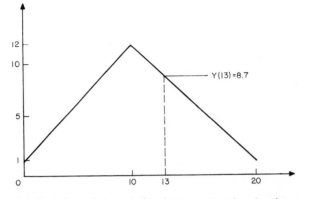

Fig. 55. Linear interpolation between two breakpoints.

SØRTFL is an initializing routine called to specify that floating-point numbers are to be sorted. The calling sequence for SØRTFL used in Pass II is simply

CALL SØRTFL

The calling sequence used in Pass II for the sort routine is

CALL SØRT (T(1), T(2), IN, I)

where T(1) and T(2) are the first two words on a list that will be sorted into monotonic increasing order, IN is the number of words to be sorted, and I is the location of the first word of a second list which will be rearranged in exactly the same manner as the T list.

In Pass II, T contains action times for data statements and I contains pointers to where the data statements begin in the D array. After sorting, the pointers in the I array will have been so rearranged that successive pointers point to data statements in the D array in their proper chronological sequence.

If two entries in the T array are equal, SØRT will *not* interchange their order. The preservation of order is essential for the data statements that define an instrument. All these have the same action time, but their order must be maintained.

14. PLS Routines

A data statement of the type

PLS AT n D4 D5 ... Dm ;

causes Pass II to execute the statement

CALL PLSn

where n is some integer between 1 and 5. The call is carried out at action time AT relative to the processing of other data statements in Pass II. PLSn is a subroutine that must be supplied by the user. It can perform any desired function, but a typical use would be to change a note parameter, such as pitch, according to some composing rule. For more information on the use of PLS routines, see the tutorial examples in Chapter 2.

The data statement PLS AT n D4 . . . is stored in numerical form in the Pass II D(10,000) array at the time the call to PLSn takes place. The arrangement is

$$D(M) = \text{word count}$$
$$D(M + 1) = 10 \quad \text{(the numerical equivalent of PLS)}$$
$$D(M + 2) = AT$$
$$\text{etc.}$$
$$M = IP(2)$$

Thus, for example, in order to find D5 from the data statement, PLS must look up M at IP(2) and then look in $G(M + 6)$. Such a roundabout procedure is necessary because of the sorting.

The dimension and common statements in Pass II and PLSn must, of course, be identical.

15. CØNVT—Convert Subroutine

This subroutine is called by WRITE2 immediately before each data statement is written out to be used as input by Pass III. It must be supplied by the user and replaces CVT functions in Music IV. Special conversion of input parameters are possible, such as converting a frequency given in cycles per second to an appropriate increment, conversion of a special amplitude notation to a form acceptable to Pass III, and so forth. Attack, steady-state, and decay times may be converted to correct increments for driving the ENV generator.

The necessary FØRTRAN CØMMØN statement is

CØMMØN IP(10), P(100), G(1000)

CØNVT is called by the statement

CALL CØNVT

At this time the parameters for the data statement are in the P array, and the number of parameters is in IP(1). G(5) and G(6) contain the starting time and duration in beats, if the metronomic scaling has been used.

CØNVT may perform complicated logical functions. It may increase or decrease the number of parameters, changing IP(1) accordingly. For more information, see the tutorial examples described in Chapter 2.

16. Description of Pass III

Pass III reads a sequence of data statements that have been ordered according to increasing action times, and it executes the operations specified by these data statements. The principal operations are defining instruments and playing notes. In addition, functions, variables, and numbers may be computed and stored in the Pass III memory for subsequent use in playing notes.

As mentioned in the introduction, most of the data in Pass III are stored in a large linear array I. Included are instrument definitions, input–output blocks for unit generators, functions, note parameters.

The size of the various parts of I will vary greatly, depending both on the specific computer being used and on the composition being played. Consequently the structure of I is described in the IP data array, which may be easily changed. Details are given in Section 17.

Over-all Operation

The over-all operation of Pass III is diagrammed in Fig. 56. The program is started by reading a few constants from IP, including the sampling rate IP(3) and the scale factor for variables IP(12).

A section is started by resetting the "played to" time T(1) to zero, since time is measured from the beginning of each section.

The main loop of Pass III consists simply of reading a data statement into the P array. As in previous passes, the P array is used exclusively for reading and processing data statements. The operation code always appears in P(1) and the action time in P(2). Samples of the acoustic output are generated until the "played to" time equals the action time. Then the operation code is interpreted and executed. The next data statement is then read and processed.

Instrument Definitions

If the operation code defines an instrument, the definition is entered in the I array starting with the first empty location in the table for instrument definitions. The location of the beginning of this instrument definition is recorded in the location table for instrument definitions. Different instruments are designated by being numbered.

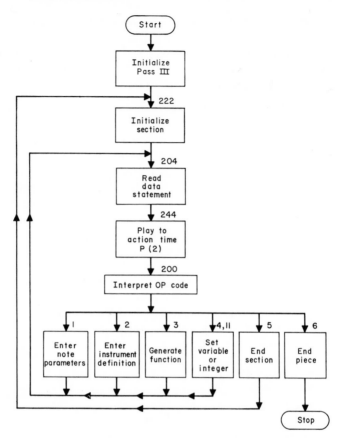

Fig. 56. Block diagram of main loop—Pass III.

An instrument definition consists of a list of the various types of unit generators used by the instrument, together with the inputs, outputs, and functions for these units. Inputs and outputs can be note parameters obtained for each note from a data statement, variables that are single numbers stored more or less permanently in the I array, or input–output blocks. These blocks are used for intercommunication between unit generators. Instrument definitions continue unchanged from one section to the next—unless they are redefined, in which case the latest definition applies.

Note Playing

If the operation code specifies a note to be played, the data from the P array are moved into the first unused block of locations in the note-parameter storage area. Unused note-parameter blocks have -1 in their first location; otherwise this location contains the instrument number. To scale amplitudes the $P(2) \rightarrow P(n)$ parameters are multiplied by IP(12) before storage in the note-parameter block (see paragraph on scale factors, p. 157). The *number* of note-parameter blocks determines the *maximum number of voices* that may be played simultaneously.

The termination time of the note is entered into the first unused location of the TI array, and the I array subscript of the note parameters is entered in the corresponding location of the ITI array. Unused locations in TI are marked with the number 1000000.0. TI and ITI are used to control the synthesis of samples of the acoustic waveform.

Play to Action Time

The most intricate part of Pass III consists in generating acoustic samples until the "played to" time T(1) equals the action time P(2) of the current data statement. In the process, any notes terminating before P(2) are turned off at their proper termination times. Several steps are involved. This part of the program is diagrammed in Fig. 57.

The action time P(2) is put in the current "play-to" objective T(2). The TI array that contains the terminating times of the instruments currently playing is searched for the minimum termination time TMIN. If TMIN $<$ T(2), acoustic samples are generated until T(1) $=$ TMIN, TMIN is removed from TI, and the whole process is repeated. If TMIN $>$ T(2), samples are generated until T(1) $=$ T(2) and control is returned to the operation-code interpreter (FØRTRAN statement 200). If TI is or becomes empty, a rest is generated until T(1) $=$ T(2). The algorithm just described starts at FØRTRAN statement 244 as indicated in Fig. 58.

The playing routines start at statement 260. The number of samples to be generated ISAM is computed as the product of the sampling rate I(4) times the time to be currently generated T(3) $-$ T(1). T(3) is the current objective for T(1). Sample generation proceeds by blocks. The length of the block is the minimum of (1) the length of a unit-generator input–output block, or (2) the number of samples remaining in ISAM. For each block of samples the program scans all note-parameter blocks (statement 268). For each voice that is turned on (first note parameter $\neq$ -1) the program scans the instrument definition specified by the first note parameter (statement 271). Each unit generator specified in the instrument definition is called in the order in which it occurs in the definition. Either SAMGEN or FØRSAM is called, depending on

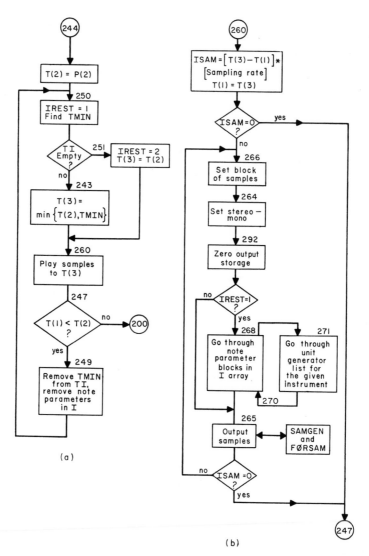

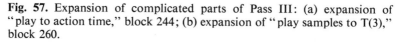

Fig. 57. Expansion of complicated parts of Pass III: (a) expansion of "play to action time," block 244; (b) expansion of "play samples to T(3)," block 260.

whether the unit-generator number is an integer less than or greater than 100.5.

After all unit generators in all instruments have produced a block of samples, the block is outputted with SAMØUT (statement 265). Another block is generated until ISAM is reduced to zero.

Function Generation

Some unit generators, in particular oscillators, use stored functions. These are computed and stored by FØRTRAN subroutines GEN1, GEN2, ... which may be supplied by the user. Existing GENn functions for computing straight-line functions and sums of sinusoids are described in Section 25. Upon reading a data statement that requests function generation, Pass III calls upon the requested function. Space to hold the functions is provided in the I array.

Scale Factors

Because FØRTRAN stores only integers in fixed-point arrays such as I, variables that are inputs to unit generators are multiplied by IP(12), which is set equal to 2^n. This is equivalent to putting the decimal point n places from the right end of the memory word. For a machine with a 36-bit word, n is typically 18. Likewise functions are multiplied by IP(15) which is typically set to $2^{35} - 1$ in a 36-bit machine.

Variable and Number Storage

The operation codes SV3, SI3, and SIA cause numbers and variables to be stored in the I array. Variable number 1 is stored at I(101), number 2 at I(102), etc. The appropriate P field is multiplied by the scale factor IP(12) before storing. Thus I(m) equals IP(12) $*$ P(n).

Integers are stored starting with integer 1 at I(1), integer 2 at I(2), etc. In general, these numbers are used to control the program. The following locations in I have special uses

I(4)   Sampling rate

I(7)   Master random number

I(8)   Mono-stereo control. I(8) = 0 for monophonic output, I(8) = 1 for stereophonic

These may be changed as desired. Otherwise I(1) through I(20) are reserved for program control and should not be changed. The SI3 and SIA operations do not use a scale factor.

Multiple-Use Instruments and Unit Generators

The structure of Pass III has been designed so that the same block of code embodying a unit generator is used in all instruments. Furthermore the same instrument can simultaneously (in the sense of time of the acoustic wave) produce many voices. This requires that no data specific to a given instrument or voice can be stored in the unit-generator code.

Note-parameter blocks in the I array are kept intact for the duration of a note. Hence certain quantities that must be continuous throughout the note, particularly SUM in the oscillator, should be kept in the note-parameter block.

Input–output blocks for unit generators must not be incorrectly overwritten inside an instrument. The same block may be used as input and output to a given unit generator, since the input is read before the output is written. However, a block cannot be used simultaneously for two different purposes, for example, as two inputs to a unit generator. That is, it should be kept in mind that an input–output block may contain only one set of values at a time (see Fig. 58).

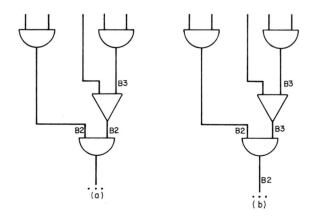

Fig. 58. Examples of (a) an incorrect and (b) a correct input–output block.

17. I and IP Data Arrays in Pass III

Most of the data in Pass III are kept in a large one-dimensional array $I(n)$. Included are instrument definitions, note parameters, functions, unit-generator input–output blocks, and a few other miscellaneous data. Except for a few fixed locations which will be listed below, the data arrangement is flexible and is determined by parameters compiled into the $IP(n)$ parameter table. IP contains the main Pass III constants which may change from time to time or from one computer to another—constants such as the number and size of the functions, scale factors for variables and functions, the sample value equal to zero pressure in the acoustic output wave, etc.

The I array is usually structured as shown in the diagram below. Values stored in IP give the subscripts in $I(n)$ at which various quantities are stored.

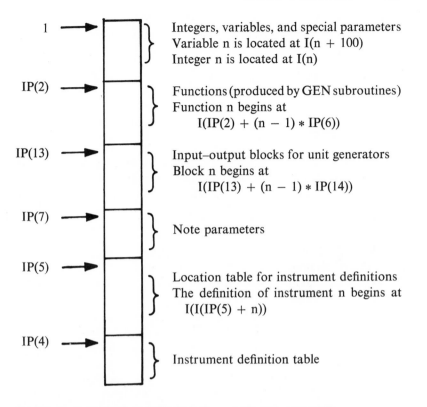

1 → Integers, variables, and special parameters
Variable n is located at I(n + 100)
Integer n is located at I(n)

IP(2) → Functions (produced by GEN subroutines)
Function n begins at
$$I(IP(2) + (n - 1) * IP(6))$$

IP(13) → Input–output blocks for unit generators
Block n begins at
$$I(IP(13) + (n - 1) * IP(14))$$

IP(7) → Note parameters

IP(5) → Location table for instrument definitions
The definition of instrument n begins at
$$I(I(IP(5) + n))$$

IP(4) → Instrument definition table

For example if IP(2) = 1000, functions will start at I(1000).

Certain special parameters in I have fixed locations and a particular meaning, as follows

I(1) Number of words on the current data statement in the P(n) array

I(2) Subscript of first empty location in instrument definitions

I(3) Subscript of note parameters for the note currently being played

I(4) Sampling rate

I(5) Number of samples to synthesize in the current group

I(6) Subscript of starting location in the instrument definition for the unit generator currently being played

I(7) Master random number

I(8) Monophonic-stereophonic signal
I(8) = 0 for monophonic; I(8) = 1 for stereophonic

Any location in the I array may be set by an SV3, SI3, or SIA operation. In the set-variable operation the scale factor for variables is used so that

$$I(n) = IP(12) \cdot P(m)$$

whereas for integers no scale factor is involved

$$I(n) = P(m)$$

The following constants are compiled into the IP(n) array. The array is constructed by a BLØCK DATA subprogram and is stored in labeled CØMMØN memory, labeled PARM.

IP(1)   Number of operation codes in Pass III
IP(2)   Beginning subscript of functions
IP(3)   Standard (default) sampling rate
IP(4)   Beginning subscript of instrument definitions
IP(5)   Beginning subscript of location table for instrument definitions
IP(6)   Length of a function
IP(7)   Beginning subscript of blocks of note-parameter storage
IP(8)   Length of a block of note-parameter storage
IP(9)   Number of blocks of note parameters (equals the maximum number of voices that can play simultaneously)
IP(10)   Subscript of unit-generator input–output block which is reserved for storage of samples of the acoustic output waveform. SAMØUT puts out samples from this block
IP(11)   Sound zero. This is integer with decimal point at right end of the word
IP(12)   Scale factor for unit-generator variables (input–outputs, etc.)
IP(13)   Subscript of beginning of unit-generator input–output blocks
IP(14)   Length of a unit-generator input–output block
IP(15)   Scale factor for functions

18. Note Parameters

The word count and parameters P1 through Pn are read by Pass III from a data statement on the input file and are initially put into I(1) and into the P array. If P1 $= 1 \equiv$ NØT, the parameters must be moved to a vacant block of note-parameter storage because other data statements will be read into the P array before the NØT is completed. Note-parameter blocks start at I(n) (n = IP(7)), each block is IP(8) locations long, and IP(9) blocks are available.

A block contains the following arrangement of the information

$$I(n) = P3 \qquad \text{(the instrument number)}$$
$$I(n + 1) = P2 * IP(12)$$
$$I(n + 2) = P3 * IP(12)$$
$$\vdots$$
$$I(n + m + 1) = Pm * IP(12)$$

All subsequent locations to end of block are filled out with zeros. All locations are in fixed-point format. All locations except the first are scaled by the IP(12) scale factor. The first location I(n) contains the instrument number, unscaled. If a block is empty, I(n) contains -1.

When a unit generator is called to calculate part of a note, $I(3) = n$ is set to the first location of the note-parameter block for that note. Consequently note parameter Pk may be found at $I(n + k - 1)$.

19. Instrument Definition

An instrument in Pass III is defined by a *sequence* of data statements, which are read from the input medium. The description is stored in the I(n) array in the instrument definition table.

The format of the input data statements in Pass III is in the following table.

Record #	Word Count	P(1)	P(2)	P(3)	
1	3	2	Action time	Inst No	
2	n	2	Action time	Unit type	$D_1 \ldots D_{n-3}$
3	n	2	Action time	Unit type	$D_1 \ldots$
...					
last	2	2	Action time		

The description is terminated by a two-word statement. The quantities D_i specify the various inputs and outputs to the unit generators.

If $D_i < -100$, then $|D_i| - 100$ is a function number
If $-100 \leq D_i < 0$, then $|D_i|$ is the number of a unit-generator input–output block
If $1 \leq D_i \leq 100$, then D_i is a note-parameter number
If $100 < D_i$, then $D_i - 100$ is a variable number

The mnemonic form of instrument definition as written on the score and read by READ1 has already been described in Section 4. Examples are given in Section 5.

The instrument definition is stored starting in $I(n)$ where $n = I(IP(5) + \text{Inst number})$. Instrument definitions are stored in successive locations in $I(n)$ according to their action times. The first unused location in the instrument definition table is kept in $I(2)$. An instrument with a given number may be redefined at any action time. The new definition will be used subsequently. However, no "garbage collection" is done and the old definition will continue to occupy space in $I(n)$.

The format of the description in $I(n)$ is as follows:

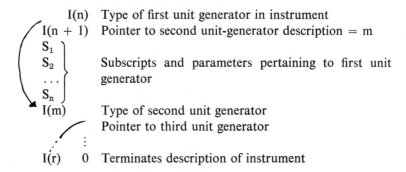

$I(n)$	Type of first unit generator in instrument
$I(n + 1)$	Pointer to second unit-generator description $= m$
S_1	
S_2	Subscripts and parameters pertaining to first unit
...	generator
S_n	
$I(m)$	Type of second unit generator
	Pointer to third unit generator
	⋮
$I(r)$ 0	Terminates description of instrument

The S_i's that specify inputs, outputs, and functions for the unit generators have the following meaning:

If $S_i < 0$, then $|S_i|$ is the subscript in I which specifies the beginning of a function or of a unit generator input–output block.
If $1 \leq S_i \leq 262{,}144$, then S_i is the number of a note-card parameter.
If $262{,}144 < S_i$, then $S_i - 262{,}144$ is the subscript in I of a variable. The number of the variable is $S_i - 262{,}144 - 100$.

20. FØRSAM

FØRSAM is a subroutine that contains unit generators written in FØRTRAN. These may be used either separately or together with SAMGEN which contains unit generators written in basic machine language.

FØRSAM is called in Pass III by the statement

CALL FØRSAM

The call causes FØRSAM to compute NSAM $(= I(5))$ samples of the output of unit generator, type J (J is given in the instrument description). Unit-generator types in FØRSAM are numbered 101 and up in order to differentiate them from SAMGEN unit generators, which are numbered 1 through 100.

The block diagram of the program is shown in Fig. 59.

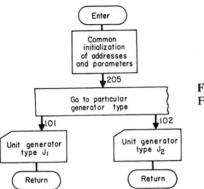

Fig. 59. Block diagram of FØRSAM program.

Computation can be made in either fixed or floating-point arithmetic. Usually the scale-factor variables, IP(12) and IP(15), will be necessary to scale the results.

A listing of a small FØRSAM program with only one unit generator is shown below. The initializing routines in the program accommodate other unit generators which can be added to the program simply by extending the GØ TØ at 205 and writing the unit-generator code.

The dimension statement includes three arrays from Pass III, I, P, and IP, and two other arrays, L and M, which are used to address the unit-generator inputs and outputs. L and M are computed by the initialization procedure.

Specifically, the jth input or output will be found at I(m) where m = L(j). M indicates whether an input or output is a single number (note parameter or variable) or a block of numbers (function or I-Ø block). If M(j) = 0, the jth input is a single number; if M(j) = 1, the jth input is a block. For blocks, L(j) gives the subscript of the first number in the block. Inputs and outputs are sequentially numbered. Thus in the data statement

    ØSC P5 P6 B2 F1 S ;

P5 is the first, P6 the second, B2 the third, F1 the fourth, and S the fifth. For more convenient referencing, an equivalence is set up so that L(i) ≡ L_i and M(i) ≡ M_i.

```
      SUBROUTINEFORSAM
      DIMENSIONI(15000),P(100),IP(20),L(8),M(8)
      COMMONI,P/PARM/IP
      EQUIVALENCE(M1,M(1)),(M2,M(2)),(M3,M(3)),(M4,M(4)),(M5,M(5)),(M6,M
     1(6)),(M7,M(7)),(M8,M(8)),(L1,L(1)),(L2,L(2)),(L3,L(3)),(L4,L(4)),(
     2L5,L(5)),(L6,L(6)),(L7,L(7)),(L8,L(8))
C     COMMON INITIALIZATION OF GENERATORS
      N1=I(6)+2
      N2=I(N1-1)-1
      DO204J1=N1,N2
      J2=J1-N1+1
      IF(I(J1))200,201,201
  200 L(J2)=-I(J1)
      M(J2)=1
      GOTO204
  201 M(J2)=0
      IF(I(J1)-262144)202,202,203
  202 L(J2)=I(J1)+I(3)-1
      GOTO204
  203 L(J2)=I(J1)-262144
  204 CONTINUE
      NSAM=I(5)
      N3=I(N1-2)
      NGEN=  N3 -100
  205 GOTO(101,300,300),NGEN
C     UNIT GENERATOR 101- INTERPOLATING OSCILLATOR
  101 SFU=IP(12)
      SFF=IP(15)
      SFUI=1./SFU
      SFFI=1./SFF
      SFUFI=SFU/SFF
      SUM=FLOAT(I(L5))*SFUI
      IF(M1)210,210,211
  210 AMP=FLOAT(I(L1))*SFUI
  211 IF(M2)212,212,213
  212 FREQ=FLOAT(I(L2))*SFUI
  213 XNFUN=IP(6)-1
      DO223J3=1,NSAM
      J4=INT(SUM)+L4
      FRAC=SUM-AINT(SUM)
  216 F1=FLOAT(I(J4))
      F2=FLOAT(I(J4+1))
  217 F3=F1+(F2-F1)*FRAC
      IF(M2)218,218,219
  218 SUM=SUM+FREQ
      GOTO220
  219 J4=L2+J3-1
      SUM=SUM+FLOAT(I(J4))*SFUI
  220 IF(SUM-XNFUN)215,214,214
  214 SUM=SUM-XNFUN
  215 J5=L3+J3-1
      IF(M1)221,221,222
  221 I(J5)=IFIX(AMP*F3*SFUFI)
      GOTO223
  222 J6=L1+J3-1
      I(J5)=IFIX(FLOAT(I(J6))*F3*SFFI)
  223 CONTINUE
      I(L5)=IFIX(SUM*SFU)
  300 RETURN
      END
```

The number of samples to be generated is put in NSAM. Most of the unit generators will operate with a loop such as DØ 223 J3 = 1, NSAM.

In the computations performed by the unit generator, it is necessary to test to see whether an input is a single number or an I-Ø block. If $M_j = 0$, the jth input need only be obtained once from $I(L_j)$. If the jth input is an I-Ø block ($M_j = 1$), then each value is obtained with the help of the main DØ index J3. For example, the third input is located at $I(J5)$ where

$$J5 = J3 + L3 - 1$$

The particular unit generator is an oscillator that interpolates between adjacent values of the function (see Section 6 for discussion of why interpolation is useful). Computations are carried out in floating-point arithmetic. Since the input data are fixed-point numbers, they must be floated and scaled by appropriate constants. Scale factors for I-Ø blocks and for functions are given in IP(12) and IP(15), respectively. The necessary scaling constants are computed at 101.

21. SAMGEN

SAMGEN is one of the few basic machine language programs in Music V. Consequently it must be written specifically for the particular machine on which it is to be used. The Bell Laboratories program is written in GMAP for a General Electric 635 computer. A few comments about the program may be of use in designing programs for other machines.

SAMGEN includes the unit generators of type numbers less than 100. The computation of the actual acoustic samples, which is the preponderance of the computation in Music V, is done by SAMGEN.

The general form of SAMGEN is shown in Fig. 60.

SAMGEN is written in such a way that one procedure can be used to set the parameters in all of its unit generators. This procedure accesses the I array in common storage during Pass III in order to find out

I(3) the subscript in the I array of the note parameters for the note being played

I(5) the number of samples to generate and

I(6) the subscript in the I array for the instrument definition table of the unit generator being played.

The procedure then reads through the instrument description for the unit generator being played. (See instrument description, Section 19.)

For each unit generator, the procedure expects a certain number of inputs (S_i's) in a certain order, e.g., if unit type = 2 (oscillator), then

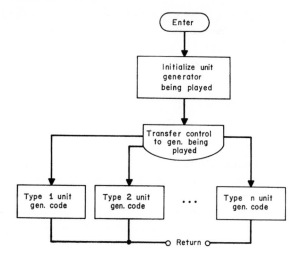

Fig. 60. Block diagram of SAMGEN program.

S_1 = amplitude, S_2 = frequency, S_3 = output, S_4 = function, and S_5 = sum. It then sets addresses in the specified unit generator according to the following conventions:

If $S_i < 0$, then $|S_i|$ is the subscript in the I array of the beginning of a function or of unit-generator I-Ø block.

If $0 < S_i < 262,144$, then S_i is the number of a note parameter. Note parameter Px is located at $I(I(3) + x - 1)$. (See Section 18 for more information on note-parameter storage.)

If $S_i > 262,144$, then $S_i - 262,144$ is the subscript in the I array of a variable: variable x is located at $I(x + 100)$.

After the addresses are initialized, SAMGEN transfers control to the specified unit generator, which generates the number of samples specified in I(5).

The calling sequence is

CALL SAMGEN

Almost all information is supplied by the I array which is located in unlabeled common storage according to the statement

CØMMØN I

SAMGEN uses no subroutines.

22. SAMØUT

SAMØUT is another GMAP subroutine called by Pass III which (1) scales samples which are ready to be output, and (2) calls FRØUT to output these samples onto magnetic tape. Samples (S_i) are scaled according to

$$S_i = S_i/2^{18} + 2048$$

The calling sequence is

CALL SAMØUT (IARRAY, N)

where IARRAY = address of first sample to be output, and N is the number of samples to be output.

Other routines used by SAMØUT are

FRØUT4

No common storage is used.

23. SAMØUT for Debugging

This version of SAMØUT (cf. Section 22) is provided for debugging purposes only. It is called by Pass III with the call

CALL SAMØUT (IARRAY, N)

in order to *print* out N samples starting from location IARRAY. It must perform the same descaling operations as the normal SAMØUT, i.e.,

$$sample_i = (sample_i/2^{18}) + 2048$$

This version of SAMØUT is written in FØRTRAN and will print the sample values in any convenient format. It is recommended that in using this version of SAMØUT one should be careful of excessive output since it is easy to ask for a very large number of acoustic samples.

24. Acoustic-Sample Output Program: FRØUT

The subroutine package FRØUT is called by both Pass III and SAMØUT in order to write the actual acoustic samples generated by Music V onto magnetic tape. FRØUT is coded in assembly language rather than FØRTRAN (1) for efficiency and (2) because it must write special physical records onto tape in a form suitable for digital-to-analog conversion. This is usually not possible in a compiler language such as FØRTRAN.

The exact form of FRØUT will depend on the particular machine configuration of a computer installation. It is therefore necessary that this program be written by an experienced programmer at any computer installation that desires to run Music V.

There follows a general description of the FRØUT programs written at Bell Telephone Laboratories for use with the General Electric GE645 computer. It should act only as a model for such a program written for another machine.

Basically FRØUT simply takes sample values that are produced by Music V, packs several samples into one computer word, and writes them onto magnetic tape in a form suitable for digital-to-analog conversion.

At BTL, the digital-to-analog converters operate with 12-bit samples. Since the GE645 computer is a 36-bit word-length machine, FRØUT packs the acoustic samples three per word.

One packed computer word is of the form

```
┌────────────── 36 bits ──────────────┐
aaaaaaaaaaaaabbbbbbbbbbbbbccccccccccccc
└ sample 1 ┘└ sample 2 ┘└ sample 3 ┘
```

Since the maximum integer value that can be represented in 12 bits is 4095_{10}, FRØUT screens the sample values it receives from Music V to be sure that it falls in the range 0 to 4095. Should any samples to be written by FRØUT be outside this range, they are clipped to 0 and 4095.

Pass III first calls FRØUT0 during its initializing sequence with the call

CALL FRØUT0 (66, 167)

where 66 is a file code (i.e., a logical file name of the tape file onto which packed acoustic samples are to be written), and 167 is the record length in 36-bit words to be written onto this tape (samples per tape record = 3 × words per tape record).

Whenever Music V has produced some samples that are ready to be output, subroutine SAMØUT is called by Pass III, which in turn calls FRØUT with the call

CALL FRØUT4 (IA, N)

which writes N samples onto tape starting from the location IA.

At the end of the composition, Pass III calls FRØUT with the call

CALL FRØUT3

FRØUT3 completes the output buffer, if it was only partially filled, with zero-voltage samples, empties this last buffer onto tape, and writes an end-of-file mark.

Packing of samples can be accomplished by machine-language shifting instructions and buffering. Acoustic sample tapes typically are unlabeled and unblocked, and use fixed-length records.

FRØUT3 prints a statement giving the number of samples out of range in the file which has just been terminated.

25. GEN—Pass III Function-Generating Subroutines

GEN1

GEN1 is a FØRTRAN subroutine to generate functions composed of segments of straight lines. The calling sequence is

CALL GEN1

Data are supplied by the P(n), I(n), and IP(n) arrays. The jth function $F_j(i)$ is generated according to the form shown in the diagram below.

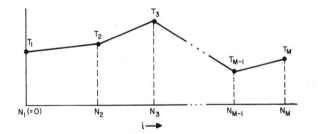

Linear interpolation is used to generate the function between M points which are specified by the user. Thus between any two abscissa points N_m and N_{m+1} the function points are computed according to the relation

$$F_j(i) = T_m + (T_{m+1} - T_m) \cdot \frac{i - N_m}{N_{m+1} - N_m} \quad i = N_m \ldots (N_{m+1} - 1)$$

The number of corners M is arbitrary and is determined by the word count I(1). $M = (I(1) - 4)/2$.

In general the user will set $N_1 = 0$ and $N_M = IP(6) - 1$, so that the number of points in the function equals IP(6).

The parameters of the function are arranged as follows:

P(1)	P(2)	P(3)	P(4)	P(5)	P(6)	P(7)	P(8)	...
3	Action time	1	Function No (j)	T_1	N_1	T_2	N_2 ...	N_M

The function is stored starting in I(n) where $n = IP(2) + (j - 1) *$ IP(6) and is scaled by IP(15) so that, for example, $I(n) = T_1 * IP(15)$.

GEN2

GEN2 is a FØRTRAN subroutine to generate a function composed of sums of sinusoids. The calling sequence is

CALL GEN2

Data are supplied by the P(n), I(n), and IP(n) arrays.

The jth function $F_j(i)$ is generated according to the relation

$$F_j(i) = (\text{amp normalizer})\left\{ \sum_{k=1}^{N} A_k \sin \frac{2\pi ki}{P - 1} \right.$$

$$\left. + \sum_{k=0}^{M} B_k \cos \frac{2\pi ki}{P - 1} \right\} \quad i = 0 \dots P - 1$$

$P (= IP(6))$ is the number of samples in a function.

The parameters for the function are arranged as follows:

P(1)	P(2)	P(3)	P(4)	P(5)	...	P(−)	P(−)
3	Action time	2	Function No (j)	A_1 ...	A_N B_0 ... B_M	$\pm N$	

The number of sine terms is $|N|$. If N is positive, amp normalizer is computed so max $|F_j(i)| = .99999$. If N is negative, amp normalizer $= .99999$. The number of cosine terms M is computed from N and the word count I(1). $M = I(1) - N - 5$.

The number of samples in the function is IP(6).

The function is stored starting in I(n), and is scaled by IP(5)

$$I(n) = IP(15) * F_j(0), \text{ etc.}$$

where $n = IP(2) + (j - 1) * IP(6)$.

The *first* and *last* samples of the function are *equal*, $F_j(0) = F_j(P - 1)$, thus the period in samples is $P - 1$.

GEN3

General description:

GEN3 is a FØRTRAN subroutine which generates a stored function according to a list of integers of arbitrary length. These integers specify the relative amplitude at equally spaced points along a continuous periodic function. The first and last points are considered to be the same when the function is used periodically (e.g., by an oscillator).

Calling sequence:

CALL GEN3

Other routines used by GEN3:

Data statement:

GEN, action time, 3, stored function number, P_1, P_2, ..., P_{nj}

Examples:

The following P_i's will generate the functions shown below.

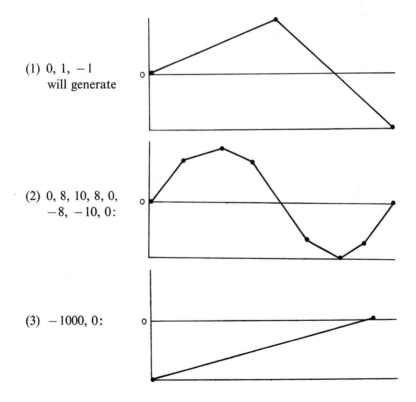

(1) 0, 1, −1
     will generate

(2) 0, 8, 10, 8, 0,
     −8, −10, 0:

(3) −1000, 0:

26. Data Input for Pass III—DATA

Subroutine DATA is called by Pass III with the call

CALL DATA

This causes one data statement to be read from file 11 into the P array in CØMMØN storage according to

READ (11) K, (P(J), J = 1, K)

I(1) is set equal to K (word count).

Annotated References by Subject

Music IV Program

M. V. Mathews, "The Digital Computer as a Musical Instrument," *Science*, *142*, 553–557 (November 1963). A semitechnical description of Music IV with some discussion of applications. This is a good introductory article.

M. V. Mathews, "An Acoustic Compiler for Music and Psychological Stimuli," *Bell Sys. Tech. J. 40*, 677–694 (May 1961). A technical description of an early version of a sound generating program. This is the first complete published description.

J. R. Pierce, M. V. Mathews, and J. C. Risset, "Further Experiments on the Use of the Computer in Connection with Music," *Gravesaner Blätter*, No. 27/28, 92–97 (November 1965). A semitechnical description emphasizing applications of Music IV. This is a good follow-up for the paper in *Science*.

J. C. Tenney, "Sound Generation by Means of a Digital Computer," *J. Music Theory*, *7*, 25–70 (1963). A discussion of Music IV as seen by a composer using the program. The article contains many details and is a good introduction for a musician.

Appendix A Psychoacoustics and Music

J. R. Pierce
and M. V. Mathews

Although the technology of electronic and computer sound generation has given us new tools of almost unlimited power for making new sounds, it has also created a new problem—the need to understand the psychoacoustics of musical perception. Sounds produced by conventional instruments are so well known that composers can proceed with the intuitions they have developed from long experience. However, no such intuitions exist for new sounds. Instead, the composer must understand the relation between the physical sound wave and how it is perceived by a hearer. Psychoacoustics addresses this question and hence has become an essential knowledge for the modern composer.

With some exceptions (Helmholtz, 1863; Plomp, 1966) original scientific work in psychoacoustics has not been directed chiefly at musical problems. Thus we must draw on a variety of sources in seeking to understand musical phenomena, and we may often wish that investigators had had music in mind.

Loudness

The perceived loudness of a sound depends on many factors in addition to its intensity. For example, in order for a pure tone or sinusoid at 100 Hz to be heard, its sound intensity must be 1000 times greater than that of a pure tone at 3000 Hz. For most of the musical

173

range the perceived loudness increases as the 0.6 power of the sound pressure (Stevens, 1961). The perceived loudness increases more slowly with sound pressure for 3000-Hz tones than it does for very low frequencies, say, 100 Hz; and in the uncomfortably loud range, tones of equal power are about equally loud. This means that as we turn the volume control up or down, the balance of loudness among frequency components changes slightly.

Masking and Threshold Shifts

A tone or a noise masks or renders us incapable of hearing a less powerful tone. A tone has a strong masking effect for tones of higher frequency and a weaker masking effect for tones of lower frequency. The frequency range of masking is greater for loud tones than for soft tones. Thus we would expect that in a musical composition some sounds might be masked and unheard when the volume is set high, whereas they would be unmasked and heard when the volume is low.

Masking can be considered as a raising of the level at which tones become audible. Some rise in the threshold persists for $\frac{1}{6}$ sec or longer after a loud tone (Licklider, 1951), but the aftereffect of a loud tone on hearing is much less than that of a bright light on seeing.

Limens or Just Noticeable Differences

Limens or jnd's of loudness and frequency have been carefully measured. They are surprisingly small. However, there is evidence that the limens are much smaller than the frequency or loudness differences that can be detected in complicated listening tasks, which are more akin to music (Plomp, 1966, p. 19). Very small differences in frequency (less than a half tone) and loudness can be detected in successive tones that are not too short.

Pitch

The pitch of a complex tone is often thought of as that of its lowest partial. However, experiments made with repetitions of various patterns of pulses (Flanagan and Guttman, 1960) and with complex tones in which the upper partials are harmonics of a frequency higher than the fundamental (Plomp, 1967) show that, although the fundamental dominates at higher frequencies, the repetition rate of the tone or of its higher partials dominates at lower frequencies. The pitch of a tone may be highly uncertain by one or more octaves; thus Shepard produced a circle of 12 tones, which when cyclically repeated give the impression of always rising in pitch, with no break (Shepard, 1964). Tones with inharmonic partials, including gongs, bells, and tones specially synthesized by computers (Mathews, 1963; Pierce, 1966) may produce a sensation of pitch; a tune can be played on them. But the pitch may not be the first partial; for example, the hum tone of a bell is not the pitch to which the bell is tuned.

Quality or Timbre of Steady Tones

The sound quality or timbre of steady tones depends on the partials. Although partials up to the sixth (and sometimes higher) can be heard individually by careful listening, we tend rather to hear an over-all effect of the partials through the timbre of the tone. A pure tone or sinusoid is thin. A combination of octave partials is bright. A tone with a large number of harmonic partials is harsh or buzzy (Pierce, 1966). In general, the timbre appears to be dissonant or unpleasant if two strong partials fall within a critical bandwidth, which is about 100 Hz below 600 Hz and about a fifth of an octave above 600 Hz (Plomp, 1966).

The timbre of a sound is strongly affected by resonances in the vocal tract or in musical instruments. These resonances strengthen the partials near the resonant frequencies. Three important formants or ranges of strengthened frequency are produced by the vocal tract; they give the qualities to vowel sounds which are identifiable independent of pitch.

Transient Phenomena

Textbooks give harmonic analyses of the sounds of various musical instruments, but if we synthesize a steady tone according to such a formula it sounds little like the actual instrument. Steady synthesized vowels do not sound like speech if their duration is long.

Temporal changes such as attack, decay, vibrato, and tremolo, whether regular or irregular, have a strong effect on sound quality. A rapid attack followed by a gradual decay gives a plucked quality to any waveform. Also, the rate at which various partials rise with time and the difference in the relative intensity of partials with loudness are essential to the quality of the sound (Risset, 1965). Indeed it is at least in part the difference in relative intensity of partials that enables us to tell a loud passage from a soft passage regardless of the setting of the volume control. This clue is lost in electronic music if the tones employed have a constant relative strength of partials, independent of volume.

The "warmth" of the piano tone has been shown to be due to the fact that the upper partials are not quite harmonically related to the fundamental (Fletcher *et al.*, 1962).

Consonance

Observers with normal hearing but without musical training find pairs of pure tones consonant if the frequencies are separated by more than the critical bandwidth (Plomp, 1966), or if the frequencies coincide or are within a few hertz of one another (in this case beats are heard). Pairs of tones are most dissonant when they are about a quarter of a critical bandwidth apart. For frequencies above 600 Hz, this is about a twentieth of an octave.

Excluding bells, gongs, and drums, the partials of musical instruments are nearly harmonic. When this is so, for certain ratios of the frequencies of fundamentals, the partials of two tones either coincide or are well separated. These ratios of fundamentals are 2:1 (the octave), 3:2 (the fifth), 4:3 (the fourth), 5:4 (the major third), and 6:5 (the minor third). Normal observers find pairs of tones with these ratios of fundamentals to be more pleasant, and intervening ratios less pleasant (Plomp, 1966).

Musical consonance and dissonance depend on many factors in addition to frequencies of partials. For example, unlike nonmusicians, classically trained musicians describe pairs of pure tones with these simple numerical ratios of frequency as consonant and intervening ratios as dissonant. The only reasonable explanation is that trained musicians are able to recognize familiar intervals and have learned to think of these intervals only as consonant.

Plomp (1966) has pointed out that, in order for complex tones to attain a given degree of consonance, low tones must be separated by a larger fraction of an octave than high tones, and he has observed that composers follow this principle.

If the partials of a tone are regularly arranged but not harmonic, the ratios of frequencies of the fundamental (or first partial) that lead to consonance are not the conventional ones (Pierce, 1966).

Combination Tones

When we listen to a pure tone of frequency f_1 and another tone of somewhat higher frequency f_2, we hear a combination tone of lower frequency $2f_1 - f_2$, even at low sound levels (Goldstein, 1967). At much higher sound levels, around 100,000 times or more the power at threshold, it is possible to hear faint frequencies $2f_1$, $2f_2$, $f_1 + f_2$, $f_2 - f_1$, etc. Combination tones are due to nonlinearities in the hearing mechanism. They can contribute to dissonance and to beats.

Reverberation

Reverberation is important to musical quality; music recorded in an organ loft sounds like a bad electronic organ. The reverberation for speech should be as short as possible; for music about 2 sec is effective. Music sounds dry in a hall designed for speech. Reverberation is not the only effect in architectural acoustics. Our understanding of architectural acoustics is far from satisfactory (Schroeder, 1966).

The Choir Effect

Many voices or many instruments do not sound like one voice or one instrument. Some experiments by the writers show that a choir effect cannot be attained by random tremolo or vibrato. It must be due to irregular changes in over-all waveform, caused by beating or head motions, or by differences in attack.

Direction and Distance

We can experience a sidedness to sound by wearing headphones fed from two microphones, but the sound seems to be inside our head. We experience *externalization* of the sound—as coming from a particular direction—only when we allow head movements in a sound field. Although we cannot detect the direction of the source of a sinusoidal tone in a reverberant room, we can detect the direction by the onset of such a tone, and we can detect the direction of clicks and other changing sounds. The first arrival of the sound dominates later reverberant arrivals in our sensing of the direction of the source; this is called the *precedence effect* (Wallach, Newman, and Rosenzweig, 1949). We can detect vertical angle of arrival, although no one is sure how this is done. We can also sense the distance of a source in a reverberant room; this sensation must depend on some comparison of the direct arrival and the reverberant sound (Gardner, 1967).

Memory and Overlearning

Most memory experiments are not done with musical sounds, but many are relevant to music.

Miller (1956) found that subjects can remember a sequence of from 5 to 9 randomly chosen digits, letters, or words. On the other hand, a good bridge player can remember every card that has been played in an entire game. Our ability to deal with stimuli depends on their familiarity or "meaning" to us. This familiarity comes about through overlearning. Overlearning has been insufficiently investigated because, although it is common in life, it is very difficult to achieve in the laboratory.

The phonemes of a language are overlearned. A subject can readily distinguish the phonemes of his own tongue, but not those of another. He can distinguish dialects of his own language, but not those of a foreign tongue. He can understand his native language in a noisy place better than he can understand a foreign language even though he is expert in it.

Conventional elements and structures in music are undoubtedly overlearned. Much of our appreciation of harmony, much of our ability to remember conventional tunes (Mozart, Haydn, and some other musicians could remember compositions heard only once) must depend on overlearning, just as our ability to use and remember language does. Performance with unfamiliar material is much poorer.

Psychological Distance; Scaling

Some psychological stimuli have the same pattern of similarity for all people. Color is one. The *psychological distance* between stimuli such as colors can be obtained by computer analysis of data expressing either the confusions that subjects make among pairs of stimuli or the numbers that they assign to the pairs to express their judgments of similarity. This kind of analysis is called multidimensional scaling. The stimuli may appear in a psychological space of one dimension (loudness does), two dimensions (color does) or three (vowels do) or more dimensions. Psychological distance is dependent on, but not proportional to, physical parameters. Thus red and violet light are of all colors the farthest apart in wavelength, and yet they look more alike—they are closer together psychologically—than the "intermediate" colors orange and blue.

Unhappily, multidimensional scaling is just beginning to be applied in the field of music (Levelt *et al.*, 1966). Further results might be enlightening. For instance, *we* is nearly *you* said backwards, and yet we perceive no similarity between the sounds of the two words. Is the retrograde of a phrase psychologically similar to the phrase, or is retrograde (in the words of Tovey) for the eye only? Transpositions certainly are psychologically close, but what about augmentations and inversions? What about changes in rhythm? What about manipulations of the tone row?

References

Flanagan, J. L., and N. Guttman, "On the Pitch of Periodic Pulses," *J. Acoust. Soc. Amer. 32*, 1308 (October 1960).

Fletcher, H., E. D. Blackham, and R. Stratton, "Quality of Piano Tones," *J. Acoust. Soc. Amer. 34*, 749 (June 1962).

Gardner, M., "Comparison of Lateral Localization and Distance for Single- and Multiple-Source Speech Signals," *J. Acoust. Soc. Amer. 41*, 1592 (June 1967), Abstract.

Goldstein, J. L., "Auditory Nonlinearity," *J. Acoust. Soc. Amer. 41*, 676–689 (March 1967).

von Helmholtz, H. L. F., *Die Lehre von der Tonempfindungen als physiologische Grundlage für die Theorie der Musik*, 1863. *On the Sensations of Tone as a Physiological Basis for the Theory of Music* (Dover, New York, 1954).

Levelt, W. J. M., J. P. van de Geer, and R. Plomp, "Triadic Comparisons of Musical Intervals," *Brit. J. Math. Statist. Psychol. 19* (Part 2), 163–179 (November 1966).

Licklider, J. C. R., "Basic Correlates of the Auditory Stimulus," in *Handbook of Experimental Psychology*, S. S. Stevens, Ed. (John Wiley & Sons, New York, N.Y., 1951).

Mathews, M. V., "The Digital Computer as a Musical Instrument," *Science 142*, 553 (November 1963).

Miller, G. A., "The Magical Number Seven, Plus or Minus Two," *Psychol. Rev., 63*, 81 (1956).

Pierce, J. R., "Attaining Consonance in Arbitrary Scales," *J. Acoust. Soc. Amer. 40*, 249 (July 1966).

Pierce, J. R., and E. E. David, *Man's World of Sound* (Doubleday, Garden City, N.Y., 1958).

Plomp, R., *Experiments on Tone Perception* (Institute for Perception RVO-TNO, Soesterberg, The Netherlands, 1966).

Plomp, R., "Pitch of Complex Tones," *J. Acoust. Soc. Amer. 41*, 1526–1533 (June 1967).

Risset, J. C., "Computer Study of Trumpet Tones," *J. Acoust. Soc. Amer. 38*, 912 (November 1965), Abstract.

Schroeder, M. R., "Architectural Acoustics," *Science 151*, 1355 (March 1966).

Shepard, R. N., "Circularity in Judgments of Relative Pitch," *J. Acoust. Soc. Amer. 36*, 2346 (December 1964).

Stevens, S. S., "Procedure for Calculating Loudness: Mark VI," *J. Acoust. Soc. Amer. 33*, 1577–1585 (1961).

Wallach, H., E. B. Newman, and M. R. Rosenzweig, "The Precedence Effect in Sound Localization," *Amer. J. Psychol. 52*, 315–336 (1949).

Appendix B Mathematics

In the body of this text an effort has been made to minimize the number and difficulty of mathematical expressions. In certain places some computations characteristic of signal theory must be done. This appendix lists the relations that are required by the text. No proofs are given, and the conditions under which the relations are true are not spelled out. They hold in a useful (and widely used way) for almost all real signals. We apologize for the strong MIT and EE accent in the mathematical language. If one has something to say, it is better to speak with an accent than to remain silent.

Fourier Series

A "not too discontinuous" function $f(x)$ with period T can be represented almost everywhere by the series

$$f(x) = \frac{a_0}{2} + a_1 \cos \frac{2\pi}{T} x + a_2 \cos \frac{4\pi}{T} x + \cdots$$

$$+ b_1 \sin \frac{2\pi}{T} x + b_2 \sin \frac{4\pi}{T} x + \cdots$$

where

$$a_i = \frac{2}{T} \int_0^T f(x) \cos \frac{2\pi i}{T} dx$$

and

$$b_1 = \frac{2}{T} \int_0^T f(x) \sin \frac{2\pi i}{T} dx$$

Fourier Transform

A "not too discontinuous" function $f(x)$ for which the integral of $f^2(x)$ exists may be transformed and inverse transformed according to the relations

$$P(\omega) = \int_{-\infty}^{+\infty} p(t)e^{-j\omega t} dt$$

$$p(t) = \frac{1}{2\pi} \int_{-\infty}^{+\infty} P(\omega)e^{j\omega t} d\omega$$

$P(\omega)$ is called the Fourier transform of $p(t)$; $P(\omega)$ is also called the amplitude spectrum of $p(t)$.

Input–Output Relations for Time-Invariant Linear Systems

The output $o(t)$ of a time-invariant linear system due to an input $i(t)$ may be written

$$o(t) = \int_{-\infty}^{+\infty} i(t - x)h(x) dx$$

where $h(x)$ is called the impulse response of the system. For realizable systems, $h(x) = 0$ for $x < 0$. The transform of $h(x)$ is called the transfer function $H(\omega)$ of the linear system and is written

$$H(\omega) = \int_{-\infty}^{+\infty} h(t)e^{-j\omega t} dt$$

The Fourier transform of the output $O(\omega)$ and the Fourier transform of the input $I(\omega)$ are related by the simple equation

$$O(\omega) = H(\omega)I(\omega)$$

Convolution Theorem

The three time functions, $x(t)$, $y(t)$, and $z(t)$, have as their respective Fourier transforms $X(\omega)$, $Y(\omega)$, and $Z(\omega)$. If z is the product of x and y

$$z(t) = x(t) \cdot y(t)$$

then

$$Z(\omega) = \frac{1}{2\pi} \int_{-\infty}^{+\infty} X(\alpha)Y(\omega - \alpha) \, d\alpha$$

If Z is the product of X and Y

$$Z(\omega) = X(\omega) \cdot Y(\omega)$$

then

$$z(t) = \int_{-\infty}^{+\infty} x(\sigma)y(t - \sigma) \, d\sigma$$

Definition of Unit Impulse

The unit impulse $\delta(t)$ can be considered the limit

$$\delta(t) = \lim_{\sigma \to 0} \frac{1}{\sqrt{2\pi}\sigma} e^{-t^2/2\sigma^2}$$

It is zero everywhere except at $t = 0$, but its integral is unity

$$\int_{-\infty}^{+\infty} \delta(t) \, dt = 1$$

Spectrum of Cos $\omega_0 t$

Although the integral of $\cos^2 \omega_0 t$ does not exist, and hence $\cos \omega_0 t$ does not have a legitimate Fourier transform, the transform $P(\omega)$ can be usefully defined as

$$P(\omega) = \pi[\delta(\omega - \omega_0) + \delta(\omega + \omega_0)]$$

Note in particular that the inverse transform

$$\frac{1}{2\pi} \int_{-\infty}^{+\infty} \pi[\delta(\omega - \omega_0) + \delta(\omega + \omega_0)]e^{j\omega t} \, d\omega = \tfrac{1}{2}[e^{j\omega_0 t} + e^{-j\omega_0 t}]$$

$$= \cos \omega_0 t$$

Autocorrelation Function and Power Spectrum

If $p(t)$ is an ergodic random function, then an autocorrelation function $\varphi(\tau)$ may be defined by the relation

$$\varphi(\tau) = \lim_{T \to \infty} \frac{1}{2T} \int_{-T}^{T} p(t)p(t + \tau) \, dt$$

More generally

$$\varphi(\tau) = E\langle p(t)p(t + \tau)\rangle$$

where $E\langle\ \rangle$ is defined in some way that makes sense for the random function $p(t)$. The power spectrum $\Phi(\omega)$ is the Fourier transform of $\varphi(\tau)$. Thus

$$\Phi(\omega) = \frac{1}{2\pi} \int_{-\infty}^{+\infty} \varphi(\tau)e^{-j\omega\tau}\, dt$$

$$\varphi(\tau) = \int_{-\infty}^{+\infty} \Phi(\omega)e^{j\omega\tau}\, d\tau$$

Note that the $\dfrac{1}{2\pi}$ factor is in the transform rather than the inverse transform.

Random Functions and Linear Systems

$H(\omega)$ is the transfer function of a linear system having an input $i(t)$ and an output $o(t)$. Let $\Phi_i(\omega)$ and $\Phi_0(\omega)$ be the power spectra of the input and output, respectively; then

$$\Phi_0(\omega) = |H(\omega)|^2\Phi_i(\omega)$$

Mean-Square Function

If $p(t)$ is a random function with autocorrelation function $\varphi(\tau)$ and power spectrum $\Phi(\omega)$, then

$$E\langle p(t)^2\rangle = \varphi(0) = \int_{-\infty}^{+\infty} \Phi(\omega)\, d\omega$$

Index